a LEISURE-PLAN book

how to make home wines and beers

FRANCIS PINNEGAR

contents

Leisure-Plan books are for pleasure and better living—the special kind of pleasure which comes from success with a rewarding hobby or pastime, or a more expert knowledge of home crafts.

Authoritative, lively, packed with up-to-date information, these books can be built into a library for the whole family.

HAMLYN
London · New York · Sydney · Toronto

introduction

Up until the time of the Industrial Revolution, most people in this country made their own wines and beers out of sheer economic necessity – and ironically enough, the reason that more and more people are now returning to this practice in our so-called age of affluence is exactly the same.

Forget the country folk-lore that is attached to making wines and beers in the home. With the advent of modern technology we are far better equipped than our forefathers to make excellent home-made wines and beers, to indulge our tastes in the stuff and still remain solvent.

Accuse me of being a Philistine if you will but I first embarked on the do-it-yourself drink venture some years ago simply because I like drinking even more than I hate the price one has to pay for it through the normal retail outlets.

I am going to assume that you are of similar mind but wondering just where to start with making your own wines and beers . . . which is why I have written this book for you.

How to make the best use of this book

The only way of learning how to make wines and beers is to actually make them. Though this may sound obvious, many books on the subject can confuse the beginner when he has constantly to refer backwards and forwards between the basic principles involved and what he is actually doing. So rather than separate theory from practice, I have dovetailed the two together so that you learn as you go along. Though this is essentially a practical book on the subject, you are less likely to make mistakes if you understand not only what you are doing but why you are doing it. In your first chapter you will learn how to make a wine from grape concentrate. This wine should compare equally and possibly better than the cheaper *vin ordinaires* that are on the market – at a cost well below 15p a bottle. But this wine will not be ready for drinking until after a year and that is a long time to wait for the first fruits of your labours. Therefore, I have followed this chapter with one on how to make beer – which will be ready to drink after a few weeks. This will ensure that you have a cheap and pleasant source of alcohol for your efforts and it will serve to fortify your patience while your wines mature.

From then onwards you can afford to be selective and go to those chapters which will show you how to produce the type of wine you prefer. For instance, if you would much rather have a red wine than a white wine, proceed to the appropriate chapter and tackle the sweet or dry version according to your tastes.

After the basic chapters I have then set out enough recipes to keep you busy for a lifetime. You should not tackle any of these recipes until you have completed the appropriate instructional chapters.

For your convenience I have divided the wine recipes into categories of taste so that you can easily refer to the type of wine you want to make – be it a sweet white, a dry red, or what have you.

What I would like you to do now is to go out and buy the recommended equipment and ingredients for Chapter 1 and then read what is involved while you are making the wine rather than reading about it beforehand. This way, everything will seem a lot clearer and you will realise just how easy it is to make wines and beers in your home.

some useful facts and figures

Comparison of weights and measures

English weights and measures have been used throughout this book. 3 teaspoons equal 1 tablespoon. The average English teacup is $\frac{1}{4}$ pint or 1 gill. The average English breakfast cup is $\frac{1}{2}$ pint or 2 gills.

When cups are mentioned in recipes they refer to B.S.I. measuring cup which holds $\frac{1}{2}$ pint or 10 fluid ounces. Three B.S.I. standard tablespoons measure approx. 2 fluid ounces.

In case it is wished to translate any of the weights and measures into their American or metric counterparts, the following notes and table give a comparison.

Liquid measure
The most important difference to be noted is that the American pint is 16 fluid ounces, as opposed to the British Imperial and Canadian pint which are 20 fluid ounces. The American $\frac{1}{2}$-pint measuring cup is therefore actually equivalent to two-fifths of a British pint. In Australia the British Imperial pint, 20 fluid ounces, is used. For measuring flowers use a pint or quart measure and press the flowers down lightly.

Metric weights and measures
It is difficult to convert to metric measures with absolute accuracy, but 1 oz. is equal to approximately 30 grammes, 1 lb. is equal to approximately 450 grammes, 2 lb. 3 oz. to 1 kilogramme. For liquid measure, approximately $1\frac{3}{4}$ British pints (35 fluid ounces) may be regarded as equal to 1 litre; 1 demilitre is half a litre ($17\frac{1}{2}$ fluid ounces) and 1 decilitre is one-tenth of a litre ($3\frac{1}{2}$ fluid ounces). 1 gallon is equal to approximately $4\frac{1}{2}$ litres.

Temperature conversion
To convert °F. to °C. subtract 32, then multiply by $\frac{5}{9}$.
To convert °C. to °F. multiply by $\frac{9}{5}$, then add 32.

Solid measure

British	American
1 lb. granulated or castor sugar	2 cups
1 lb. Demerara sugar	$2\frac{1}{2}$ cups
12 oz. honey	1 cup
12 oz. malt extract	1 cup
1 lb. raisins, seeded	$2\frac{3}{4}$ cups
1 lb. sultanas	$2\frac{3}{4}$ cups
$\frac{1}{4}$ oz. hops	1 cup
4 oz. crushed malt	1 cup
1 oz. flaked maize	1 cup
1 lb. dates, stoned	$2\frac{1}{2}$ cups
1 lb. dried figs, chopped	$2\frac{1}{3}$ cups
6 oz. whole almonds	1 cup
1 lb. rice	$2\frac{1}{2}$ cups
3 oz. ground coffee	1 cup
1 lb. oatmeal	$2\frac{2}{3}$ cups

Some terms and ingredients used in wine and beer-making

Air lock or fermentation lock A device used during fermentation to protect the wine from bacterial contamination. It excludes air and allows carbon dioxide to escape.

Alcohol A clear liquid produced during fermentation, giving wines and spirits their characteristic flavour.

Bottoms or lees The deposits of yeasts and solids formed during fermentation.

Bouquet The aroma of a wine.

Campden tablet A small tablet used for sterilising the equipment and preserving the wine.

Carbon dioxide The gas given off during fermentation.

Citric acid Essential for fermentation and provides the right acidity for the yeast.

Enzymes Secreted by the yeast cells during fermentation and cause changes in the substances around them.

Fermentation The process of converting a sugar solution due to yeast activity, into alcohol and carbon dioxide.

Finings Used for removing suspended solids from hazy wine or beer.

Fortification The addition of alcohol to wine as in the making of sherry or port.

Glucose A fermentable sugar, bought as glucose chippings, used in beer-making to add flavour to pale beers.

Gypsum An important constituent of water for beer-making. Helps to confer a clean dry flavour to the beer.

Hops Used in beer-making for their preservative qualities and to confer bitterness to a beer.

Hydrometer An instrument used for measuring the sugar content of a given liquid.

Macerate The action of bruising flower petals and mashing fruit.

Must The name given to a solution before it is converted into wine.

Nutrient Nitrogenous matter, usually bought in tablet form, used to boost the action of the yeast.

Pitching Adding yeast to the wort to cause fermentation in beer-making.

Priming Adding a small quantity of sugar to beer to make it sparkling.

Racking Siphoning off a clear wine or beer from the deposit into a fresh jar.

Specific gravity The weight of a liquid compared specifically to that of water.

Starter bottle A bottle containing fruit juice, water, sugar and yeast which is left in a warm place to ferment for 2–3 days.

Tannin An essential substance for a well balanced wine. It gives a 'bite' to the wine.

Wort The liquid extract consisting mainly of starchy matter before fermentation into beer.

Yeast The fermenting agent in wine and beer-making. Microscopic organisms that transform a sugary solution into an alcoholic beverage.

chapter 1

making wine from grape concentrate

Chapter 1 Making wine from grape concentrate—
Don't let's hang around. You cannot make wine until you have the necessary equipment and ingredients.

Where from? Most branches of Boots, the chemists, carry a fairly comprehensive stock. Or you can get a better selection from specialist retailers. See if you have one in your area by looking up the Yellow Pages of your local Telephone Directory.

Take this book with you when you go shopping and make sure you get all the equipment and ingredients listed before you start.

Equipment

A large saucepan This you may have already. But it is best to get a really large one with an 8-pint capacity which can also be used when you make beer.

Plastic funnels Choose one with a 5-inch diameter for filling the jars and a 2½-inch diameter one for filling bottles.

Glass fermentation jars Get the ones that hold just over a gallon. You will need two of these for each gallon of wine you make.

Long handled wooden spoon to stir things up.

Fermentation locks and bored corks to keep your jars of wine under cover while fermenting.

Corks for the jars when fermentation is finished.

Hydrometer and sample jar to tell you what is happening to the wine.

Thermometer for testing temperature of liquids.

1-pint glass measuring jug for measuring out liquids.

Kitchen scales for weighing sugar.

12-fluid ounce bottle for making fermentation starter.

4 feet rubber or polythene tubing for siphoning wine from one jar to another.

Wine bottles and labels – but these can wait until later.

Corks and seals for bottles.

Cotton wool for plugging.

Ingredients

Campden tablets for sterilisation of equipment and preserving wine.

All-purpose wine yeast and any other kind of wine yeast that catches your fancy.

Yeast nutrient tablets to help the yeast along.

½-gallon can grape concentrate – red or white – whichever you prefer – or both.

Grape tannin which is present in grape skins, but not in the concentrate.

Citric acid to provide the right acidity for the yeast.

Granulated sugar a few pounds at hand for the sweeter wines.

Oranges at least 2 for the fermentation starter.

Some of the explanations as to why you need the different equipment and ingredients may, at this stage, mean little or nothing to you.

So let's start right at the beginning.

Starting with the yeast

Yeasts are the organisms that transform a sugary solution into an alcoholic beverage – God bless them. They give up carbon dioxide in the process and leave the best part behind. Yeasts perform this mighty function of making alcohol from a very small size: twenty five thousand of them shoulder-to-shoulder might just about make up an inch.

There are a great many different kinds of yeasts . . . some of which produce horrible flavours and others which are the driving forces behind great wines. Over the years, the yeasts which are most suitable for making wines have been isolated in the laboratory. So today there are a number of pure wine yeasts available: Champagne, Burgundy, Sauternes, Pommard – to name but a few – each helping to confer a distinctive flavour to a particular wine. The All-purpose wine yeast is, as its name implies, suitable for many wines. This is the one which we will be using most.

But you can, if you wish, use a Chablis yeast for making a dry white wine, a Sauternes for a sweet white wine and a Burgundy or Pommard for a red wine.

There are four essential virtues that these wine yeasts share which make them so useful to us in making a wine:

1. They have a good head for alcohol; they can take up to about 17% of alcohol in the wine before it knocks them out.

2. They form a firm sediment after fermentation so that the wine clears well.

3. They are persistent; they keep forming alcohol for weeks on end.

4. They do not produce any nasty side flavours, if removed, after they have done their job.

These yeasts are available in a number of different forms – as tablets, liquids, cultures or granules. But in these forms they are dormant and you want to make sure that they are fully awake and raring to go when you make your wine so that you get a really vigorous fermentation. To do this, you first mix the yeast into a fermentation starter, two or three days before it is needed. By growing the yeast in a fermentation starter, the yeast multiplies millions of times, giving you a really potent brew to start fermentation in top gear.

Some ingredients and equipment for wine-making
1 *Wine bottles* **2** *Bottle brushes* **3** *Bored corks* **4** *Polythene pail* **5** *Tubing for racking wine* **6** *Wooden spoon* **7 and 15** *Plastic funnels* **8** *Saucepan* **9** *Hydrometer* **10** *Glass fermentation jar* **11** *Starter bottle* **12** *Measuring jug* **13** *Foil caps* **14** *Corking machine* **16** *Granulated sugar* **17** *Record cards* **18** *Labels* **19** *Plastic stopper* **20** *Fermentation lock* **21** *Campden tablets* **22** *Yeast nutrient tablets* **23** *Fermentation lock* **24** *Grape concentrate* **25** *Dried wine yeast* **26** *Pectic enzyme* **27** *All-purpose yeast* **28** *Tokay yeast* **29** *Cotton wool for plugging starter bottle* **30** *Grape tannin*

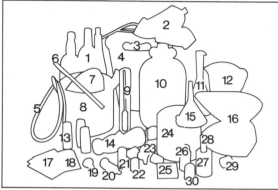

Making the fermentation starter

When making the fermentation starter, antiseptic precautions need to be taken which would seem more applicable to a hospital than a kitchen. The reason is much the same – there are lots of wild yeasts and bacteria floating around in the air and lurking on utensils which can infect the fermentation starter and spoil the wine. *Mycoderma acetii* – the vinegar bacteria – present a real and obvious danger since they can turn wine into vinegar. Sterilisation precautions, as you will learn, need to be taken not only at this stage but at all stages in making a wine.

This is what you do to make a fermentation starter.

Sterilise a plug of cotton wool in a moderately hot oven (375°F., Gas Mark 5).

Sterilise a 12-fluid ounce bottle with boiling water.

To 6 tablespoons freshly squeezed orange juice, add an equal amount of water, bring to the boil in a saucepan and then add 1 oz. sugar. Mix well until sugar is dissolved.

Pour the orange juice and sugar solution into the sterilised bottle and immediately plug with the sterilised cotton wool.

Leave the bottle and its contents to cool.

Add the yeast and replace the cotton wool plug. Leave in a warm place (about 65°F.) to ferment for 2–3 days.

Note: Yeast activity is inhibited by temperatures a little above 65°F. and the yeast cells can be killed by hot solutions. Do not take any chances over temperature – be patient and allow the solution to cool.

Remember to make up this fermentation starter 2–3 days before you start the next stage.

This method of making up a fermentation starter is also very economical. You should use about three-quarters of it to activate the ingredients for your wine and keep a quarter back. You can top up this remainder with orange juice, water and sugar – as before – and it will be ready for use again in about a week. The same yeast culture can be activated time and time again in this manner so you do not have to keep on buying more yeast.

Preparing the must

'Must' is the name given to the solution which is to be fermented and for our purposes consists basically of a solution of grape juice and sugar.

Ingredients for preparing the fermentation starter

The fermentation starter off to a good start

7

The sugar content of the must, prior to fermentation, determines whether you end up with a dry, a medium or a sweet wine. The sugar content of the grape concentrate can vary although grapes contain more sugar than practically any other fruit. But with the production of sweeter wines, more sugar needs to be added. The question is when, how much and in what dilution of water? When making the wine, we could blindly follow the instructions on the can of grape concentrate – and learn nothing. At this stage it is far better to master the basic principles of specific gravity and apply these, with the aid of a hydrometer, to working out the correct proportions of sugar and water. This is fundamental to your knowledge of making wines.

Specific gravity and the use of the hydrometer

Water has a specific gravity of 1.000. Grape concentrate has a specific gravity which is considerably higher than this – usually in the region of 1.400. It is usual practice, however, to ignore the decimal point and the figure before it and refer to just *gravity*. For example, a specific gravity of 1.400 becomes a gravity of 400; a specific gravity of 1.065 becomes a gravity of 65; and a specific gravity of 1.005, becomes a gravity of 5.

With the must, the gravity indicates the amount of sugar present. The must for a dry wine should have a gravity of 90–100; a medium wine, a gravity of about 120; and sweet wines a gravity ranging from 140–160.

It is very easy to determine the gravity of the must and hence the sugar content by using a hydrometer. The picture shows how this is done. Pour some of the must into a glass cylinder, float the hydrometer in it and read off the figure from the scale on the stem where it is level with the surface of the liquid.

The reading will be correct when the temperature of the liquid is 60°F. A difference of 10°F. either way makes no difference for practical purposes. At higher temperatures, however, the readings can be alarmingly inaccurate.

Having acquainted yourself with these principles, you can now prepare the must. But first you have to measure up and then sterilise the equipment.

Measuring up

When making a gallon of wine you will find it a great help to make a mark on the fermentation

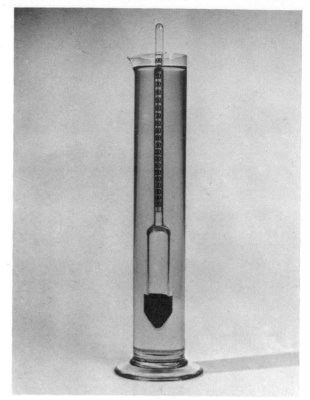

Taking a hydrometer reading

The fermentation jar marked up to the 1-gallon level

jar, indicating the exact 1-gallon level. The easiest way is as follows.

Get a pint milk bottle or measuring jug, fill it with water eight times and pour the water into the fermentation jar. Mark the level with a blob of nail varnish, paint or a strip of Elastoplast.

Sterilisation of equipment

The best way of sterilising equipment is to use sulphite in the form of Campden tablets dissolved in water. Campden tablets are composed of sodium metabisulphite and they liberate sulphur dioxide – a powerful germicidal – in water.

Campden tablets are also used in the must and wine for reasons that are explained later.

Sterilise equipment as follows.

Crush 10 Campden tablets with the back of a wooden spoon and dissolve in $\frac{1}{2}$ pint cold water. Rinse the fermentation jar with the solution; immerse the funnel, fermentation lock and cork in the solution.

Drain them thoroughly on a clean surface washed down with the solution, before use.

Decanting the grape concentrate

Boil up some water in a saucepan large enough to take the can of grape concentrate.

Open the can of grape concentrate, take out a couple of spoonfuls to allow for heat expansion and put aside to add later.

Remove the saucepan of boiling water from the heat, stand the can in it and stir with a wooden spoon until it is fluid enough to pour easily.

Pour the contents of the can into the sterilised fermentation jar, using the funnel.

Diluting the concentrate

Measure 2 pints water into a saucepan, bring to the boil and then allow to cool until tepid.

Stir in the remaining grape concentrate and then pour the whole lot through the funnel into the fermentation jar.

Keeping records

Before going any further, get out a piece of paper or an exercise book and make a note of what you are doing. It is going to be about a year before the wine is ready for drinking and it simply will not do to rely on your memory as to what you did, when you did it and what the various hydrometer readings were. The picture shows you how to keep records.

Measuring the gravity of the diluted concentrate

Mix the diluted grape concentrate thoroughly and then pour a sample into the hydrometer cylinder.

Measure the gravity with the hydrometer, make a note of the reading and return the sample to the jar.

This gives you an accurate check on the gravity of the grape concentrate. Supposing the reading was 1.200. The concentrate has been diluted by exactly one-half so you know that the gravity of the grape concentrate is 400.

Note:

Do not be confused if you see a figure expressed in Beaume on the side of the can of grape concentrate. This figure refers to the first two figures after the decimal point of specific gravity. Hence, 40 Beaume is a gravity of 400.

The steps that have been described so far apply to the production of any wine from a can of grape concentrate. Prior to fermentation and afterwards, subsequent additions vary for different types of wine and these are now described separately.

Preparing the must for a dry white wine

As was stated earlier, the gravity of the must for fermentation should be between 90–100. Supposing the gravity of the diluted grape concentrate was 200. A further dilution of these 4 pints of diluted grape concentrate with another 4 pints of water will produce a gravity of 100 – which is just about right.

So measure out another 4 pints water, bring to the boil and allow to cool before pouring into the

Keeping records

9

fermentation jar. Take a gravity reading and record it.

Preparing the must for a sweet white wine

Here, the gravity needs to be 140 or more. If you were to dilute the 4 pints grape concentrate and water solution, with say a gravity of 200, with a further 4 pints water you would have a gravity of 100. So you need to raise the gravity by at least 40 to produce a sweet white wine.

Now here is an important conversion figure to commit to memory: 2½ oz. sugar per 1 gallon will raise the gravity by 5. So 8 × 2½ oz. sugar will raise the gravity to the required figure of 40; and another 8 oz. sugar will give you a really sweet wine with a gravity of just under 160.

However the sugar is not added until after the primary fermentation for reasons that will be described later. And when added it is made up into a syrup with water.

At this stage add another 2 pints of cooled, boiled water to the fermentation jar before fermenting, take a gravity reading and record it.

Preparing the must for a medium red wine

For palatability, red wines should not be as dry as white wines. So in this case make the gravity of the must in the region of 120. If the gravity of the 4 pints grape concentrate and water solution was 200, further dilution with another 4 pints water would give a gravity of 100. You need to raise the gravity by 20. Since 2½ oz. sugar per 1 gallon raises the gravity by 5, 4 × 2½ oz. sugar will raise the gravity by 20.

At this stage add 2 pints cooled, boiled water to the fermentation jar before fermenting, take a gravity reading and record it.

Note: As an exercise in making wine, I would advise that you tackle making a medium red and/or a sweet white wine, if you were contemplating just making the dry. Even if it is not to your taste, you will gain valuable knowledge on how to work out sugar additions which will stand you in good stead – even when making other dry wines given later in this book.

Factors for fermentation of the must

Yeast This should be introduced to the must in a state of active fermentation. That is why the fermentation starter is made up and left in a warm place for 2–3 days.

Acid For the yeast cells to thrive and multiply, they need to work in an acid solution. Grape concentrate contains some acid but this has to be supplemented in the white wine concentrate with a little citric acid.

Yeast nutrient Yeasts need nitrogen and oxygen. This is supplied by adding a yeast nutrient tablet or crystals.

Sugar Ordinary granulated sugar is a sucrose which cannot be fermented by the yeast until it has been split by an enzyme secreted by the yeast into fructose and glucose – which are known as invert sugars. The sugar present in grape concentrate is invert sugar and in a state where is can be immediately worked on by the yeast to produce alcohol.

If too much sugar is present in the must during the primary fermentation, it may not all be converted into alcohol and the wine produced can be weak and sickly. This is why sugar is added at a later stage in making wine so that the yeast can convert as much as possible into alcohol.

Other additions at the beginning of fermentation

Campden tablet Grape concentrate, as with all fruits, can oxidise in the must and spoil the flavour of the wine. Sulphite, in the form of Campden tablet, prevents oxidation.

Tannin This is found naturally in grape skins but is deficient in grape concentrate. Tannin improves the flavour of the wine so some is added to the must.

Fermenting the dry wine

Add three-quarters of the fermentation starter, 1 yeast nutrient tablet, 1 Campden tablet, 6 drops grape tannin and 2 teaspoons citric acid. Shake the jar well and lightly plug with sterilised cotton wool. Stand in a warm place (about 65°F.) for 3 days.

Fermenting the sweet white wine

As for the dry wine, using only 1 teaspoon citric acid.

Fermenting the red wine

As for the dry white wine, omitting the citric acid – enough acid is already present.

Preparing the fermentation lock

The fermentation lock or air lock, protects the must from stray yeasts and bacteria in the air while it is fermenting. Also by cutting down the supply of oxygen from the outside air, the yeast obtains its supply from the sugar. The yeast thus uses more sugar and makes more alcohol.

To prepare the fermentation lock for use:

Pour a little sterile solution, composed of 1 Campden tablet dissolved in 1 pint water, into the lower part of the stem.

Insert the cork with fermentation lock into the fermentation jar.

Conducting the primary fermentation

For the first couple of days, fermentation can be extremely vigorous. But for the first few hours, little may appear to be happening and you may start twitching like an expectant father. Then you see the first few bubbles forming on the surface and within a short space of time it is bubbling away merrily.

When the first vigorous fermentation dies down you can insert the fermentation lock. After this you can happily forget the wine for a few weeks, providing the jars are not in too hot or too cool a place (65°F. is about right), while the yeast gets to work on the must, converting sugar into alcohol and bubbling off carbon dioxide.

Sugar addition for the sweet white and red wine

Sugar should not be added directly to the must since any undissolved sugar left at the bottom will weaken the yeast.

The best way to add sugar is as an inverted syrup, so that it is completely dissolved and in a form that the yeast can get to work on immediately. This is made by boiling granulated sugar and a little citric acid in water.

This is when and how you do it.

For the sweet white wine

Wait for the gravity to drop to about 100 before adding the sugar.

Make up a syrup by boiling the required amount of sugar – from 1 lb. 2 oz. to 1 lb. 10 oz. – and

Pouring a little sterile solution into the fermentation lock

An actively-fermenting must from grape concentrate

Ingredients for making the syrup

Siphoning: Inserting the tubing and sucking until the wine begins to flow
Siphoning: The wine flowing into the second jar
Siphoning: All the wine transferred to the second jar and the sediment left behind

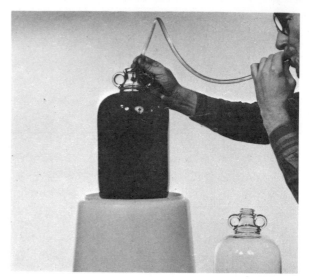

$\frac{3}{4}$ teaspoon citric acid in 2 pints water for 15 minutes.

Allow to cool thoroughly before adding to jar and replacing fermentation lock.

For the red wine

Wait for the gravity to drop to about 20 before adding the sugar.

Make up a syrup by boiling the required amount of sugar – about 10 oz. – and $\frac{1}{2}$ teaspoon citric acid in 2 pints water for 15 minutes.

Allow to cool thoroughly before adding to jar and replacing fermentation lock.

Stages of fermentation

The first few weeks of fermentation, when the yeasts are vigorous, is called the primary fermentation.

The secondary fermentation is slower and goes on for some months.

As fermentation nears completion, the wine begins to settle in layers (see picture). When gas no longer bubbles through the fermentation lock you will know that fermentation has come to an end. The wine will now clear and a thick sediment of dead yeast cells and other solids (lees) will form at the bottom of the jar. If all has gone well the gravities of the wines will be as follows and these you should check.

Dry white wine: 10 or below.

Sweet white wine: around 20.

Hard-forming sediment after fermentation

Red wine: about 15.

You are now ready to conduct the next stage in making a wine which is called *racking*.

Racking

This is the process of transferring clear or clearing wine from a jar containing sediment into a clean jar. If you let a wine stand for too long on its sediment off-tastes can develop.

This is what you do.

Clean and sterilise a second 1-gallon jar (mark the 1-gallon level) and the rubber or plastic tubing, with Campden solution, as before.

Use the rubber tubing to siphon off the wine into the prepared jar, leaving behind the sediment (see picture). Do this by putting the jar to be siphoned at a higher level than the second jar. Then insert the tube half way down the jar, suck until wine begins to flow then pinch the end with your finger and put the end in the lower bottle. On releasing your finger the wine will flow. Take care not to let the end of the tube get too near the sediment or you will suck it into the new jar.

When all the clear wine has been transferred, add 1 Campden tablet, dissolved in a little water, and top up the jar with cooled, boiled water.

Cork the jar tightly with a sterilised cork and put away in a cool, dark place to clear.

Second racking

Up to about 3 months after the first racking a second deposit will have formed and the wine on top should be bright and clear. It is then ready for its second racking. This should be carried out exactly as with the first racking, remembering to top up with cooled, boiled water. If the wine is still cloudy after another 3 months, rack again – but this is usually not necessary.

Bottling

After the wine has been maturing for six months and is perfectly clear, it is ready for bottling. You should use clear bottles for white wines and green bottles for red wines – this helps preserve the colour.

Proceed as follows.

If you are using used wine bottles, wash them out with a detergent (use a bottle brush, if necessary) and rinse thoroughly under running water.

Rinse the bottles with a Campden solution (see page 9) and allow the bottles to drain for half an hour before using.

Wine topped up with cooled, boiled water after racking

Place the corks in the sterilising solution overnight, using a weight to keep them down and completely covered; rinse and drain well before using. Always use new corks.

Siphon the wine into a sterilised jug and then use a sterilised funnel to pour the wine into the bottles. Alternatively, you can siphon the wine directly into the bottles. Fill the bottles until there is a gap of little more than $\frac{1}{2}$ inch under the cork.

Insert softened corks with a mallet and cover with a plastic or foil cap.

A much easier method is to use a corking machine (see picture).

These wines will not be ready for drinking until after a year. The sweet white wine can do with keeping even longer.

Right: A home-made wine ready for drinking
Left: Inserting the cork with a corking machine

13

Faults that can occur — how to avoid or correct them

If you have followed the instructions to the letter, nothing should really go wrong. However, it is easy enough to make mistakes, in which case, you could have trouble.

Fermentation stops too soon

1. If you forgot to add nutrient or acid, the fermentation will stick. Add the nutrient or acid and a fresh yeast starter.
2. If the must becomes too warm or too cool, this can result in fermentation sticking. The answer is to move the jar to an appropriately warmer or cooler place.
3. If too much carbon dioxide is present, this can also cause the fermentation to stick. If you suspect this, pour the must into a clean jar as vigorously as possible so that the wine becomes aerated. Also add yeast nutrient.

Unpleasant flavours develop

1. Dirty utensils can cause this.
2. Infrequent or insufficient rackings can be another cause. Do not let the wine stand too long on its sediment of dead yeast cells.

Wine becomes vinegary

Once this happens there is not much you can do but pour the wine down the sink and cleanse the jar thoroughly with Campden solution. This will not happen if you keep the must and wine well covered and observe the required sterilisation precautions.

Wine becomes 'ropey'

This very rarely happens but when it does you will certainly know. The wine becomes silky and shiny and when poured looks oily. It is caused by *lacto-bacilli* infection. However, it is easily counteracted.
Crush 2 Campden tablets and beat them well up in the wine. Store for a week, corked, and then rack into a second sterilised jar.

Important points to note

Wash all utensils and equipment as soon as you have finished with them.
Use a suitable wine yeast.
Always test the gravity of the must and keep suitable records.
Never add sugar in the solid state; always in the form of syrup.
Do not have too much sugar present for the initial fermentation.
Rack your wine at suitable intervals, and add a Campden tablet, crushed and dissolved in a little water, at each racking.
Top up with cooled, boiled water after racking.
Do not bottle your wine until it is completely stable.

chapter 2
making a beer

Note: You should acquaint yourself thoroughly with the contents of Chapter 1 before starting this chapter. Much of the information contained there is fundamental to your appreciation of what is involved here.

It is doubtful whether many people under the age of thirty know what a really good country-type beer tastes like, now that most of the smaller breweries have disappeared and been swallowed up by the larger combines. Generally speaking, the net result is a standard of uniformity and ordinariness, particularly with the increasing accent on keg beers. But one gets used to these commercial brews in the same way that one can get used to anything. So a really good home brew may taste rather strange to the uninitiated. As an analogy, it would be rather like the taste of fresh vegetables straight out of the garden to someone who has been brought up exclusively on frozen and canned produce.

What is beer?

Beer is fermented starchy matter which is drunk whilst it is still fermenting. Whereas wine is made from a must containing sugars, beer is made from a *wort* consisting mainly of starchy matter which is converted into sugar through the action of enzymes present in malt. Malt is made from barley which has sprouted.

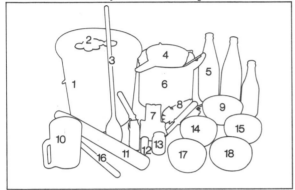

The wort is very rich in yeast food so that when the yeast is added there is soon a very vigorous fermentation. With wines the starting gravity of the must is 90 or more; with beers the starting gravity of the wort is much lower – ranging from between 30 and 60.

Different kinds of beers

Before making some beers, let us be sure of what we mean when we refer to them.

Bitter, light or pale ale A dry, light-coloured beer with a bitter taste imparted by extra hops.

Some ingredients and equipment for beer-making **1** *Polythene pail* **2** *Caps* **3** *Long handled wooden spoon* **4** *Nylon sieve* **5** *Beer bottles* **6** *Large saucepan* **7** *Crown corking machine* **8** *Bottle brushes* **9** *Granulated sugar* **10** *Mug of home-made beer* **11** *Rolling pin* **12** *Lager yeast* **13** *Granulated beer yeast* **14** *Hops* **15** *Glucose chippings* **16** *Thermometer* **17** *Flaked Barley* **18** *Crushed malt*

Make the beer that suits you best

Though there are literally hundreds of recipes for beers, there is no such thing as 'the best one'. It is all a matter of taste. Maybe you like a mild beer or a very bitter one or a stout or a lager. I have given more recipes later on in the book but if you are a keen beer drinker I urge you to experiment with different quantities and techniques. Whilst you are doing this, you should make a careful record of the ingredients you use, the quantities and every single physical factor. Then, when you hit upon a beer you really like, you should have no difficulty in reproducing it to a fair degree of consistency.

Mild or brown ale A sweet, brown beer which is made with less hops than pale ale.

Stout A dark beer which owes its colour to the presence of roasted malt grains.

Milk stout A stout made sweet by the addition of lactose (milk sugar).

Lager A dry, light-coloured beer which is brewed with a bottom fermenting yeast as opposed to a top fermenting yeast which is used for other beers.

Equipment

You will need all the equipment listed in Chapter 1, page 5, with the exception of the wine bottles, corks and seals, *plus*:

2-gallon polythene pail with lid (mark it to the 1-gallon level, if not indicated) for fermenting the wort.

Rolling pin for cracking malt.

Nylon sieve for straining the wort.

Clinitest kit for checking sugar content prior to bottling.

Beer bottles Never use bottles other than proper beer bottles or cider bottles. Otherwise the bottles can be positively lethal and go off like a bomb. Screw-top beer or cider bottles are excellent but increasingly difficult to get. If the rings on the stoppers are perished, you can replace them with new rings – your equipment shop can supply them.

Crown corking machine and caps for bottling with ordinary beer bottles if you cannot get the screw-top bottles.

Bottle brushes for cleaning.

Ingredients

This chapter gives you a choice of making one of four different kinds of beers – bitter, mild, stout or lager. The ingredients needed for each are:

Malt extract for making bitter, mild ale, stout and lager.

Crystal malt for making bitter, mild ale and stout.

Patent black malt for making stout.

Flaked maize for making mild ale and lager.

Flaked barley for making stout.

Pale ale water treatment for making bitter.

Mild ale water treatment for making mild ale and stout.

Granulated sugar for making bitter, mild ale, stout and lager.

Glucose chippings (optional) for making bitter.

Caramel for making mild ale.

Granulated beer yeast for making bitter, mild ale and stout.

Lager yeast for making lager.

Why the various ingredients are used

Malt extract This is made from barley – the fundamental ingredient in beer-making.

When barley is allowed to sprout and then dried you have what is termed as malt. The sprouting of barley causes enzymes to be produced which convert a great deal of the starch into sugar.

The malt extract which is used in home brewing is produced by sprouting barley, extracting it and evaporating off the water to produce a thick syrupy liquid. Malt extract is a convenient form of malt for use by the beginner, producing very palatable beers. Making beer from malt alone, as is practised by breweries, calls for more advanced techniques which are dealt with in Chapter 21, page 72. Make sure you use the brands of malt extract that are specially produced for home brewing.

Malt A number of different kinds of malt (malted barley) are available to the home brewer. *Crystal malt* gives more colour than the paler malts plus a roundness of flavour. *Patent black malt* adds the distinctive colour and flavour that is required of a stout and is made from burnt malts.

Cereals These are sometimes added to give beer more body. *Flaked maize* is used in light and mild beers and to some extent in lagers. *Flaked barley* helps give body and a crisp grainy taste to beer. If you like a thinner beer, the cereals can be left out.

Hops These confer bitterness to a beer but their prime function originally was to act as a preservative. There are a number of different varieties.

Fuggles and *Goldings* are the most commonly used. Goldings hops have a delicate flavour and

Extracting the hops

are used for pale beers. Fuggles hops have a stronger flavour and are used in small quantities for mild ales. You can buy these compressed or loose, in packets, but the hops have to be boiled in water to extract their flavour. Alternatively, you might try using hop extract but my own preference is for the real thing.

Sugar This, in its several forms, is fermented in beer and converted to alcohol, in addition to the starchy matter. *Glucose chippings* help confer a dryness and an added flavour to pale beers which you might or might not prefer. *Caramel* is a burnt sugar which is sometimes used in small quantities to impart a fuller flavour and colour to darker beers.

Water and mineral salts In brewing parlance, water is termed *liquor*. It is considered as one of the most important factors in brewing. The salts contained in water give beer certain characteristics. Sometimes there is a surplus of salts which has to be reduced; sometimes there is a deficiency which has to be made good.

The bitter beers and pale ales from Burton are famous and perhaps the most important reason for this is that the water contains a high proportion of calcium sulphate (gypsum) and a low proportion of chloride. This helps confer a clean, dry flavour to the beer.

A quite different kind of water is needed for mild beers and stouts. Here, a high proportion of sodium chloride (table salt) and a low proportion of sulphate is needed to bring out the full flavour.

It may be that the water from your tap is suitable for one type of beer and not another. Your local Water Board or home brewing stockist can put you in the picture and then you can condition the water with the appropriate formulations, using the manufacturer's recommended quantities. The treatment should be made at the very beginning.

Beer yeasts There are two main types of beer yeast:

1. The top fermenting yeasts which are characteristic of British brewing practice.

2. The bottom fermenting yeasts which are used for lagers and are typical of Continental brewing practice.

Each type affects the properties and the palate of the finished beer in different ways.

The top fermenting yeasts have a characteristic action. They form a thick, frothy mass on the surface of the wort within a few hours of them being added. It is necessary to skim the froth off to prevent the yeast cells dropping down into the beer and spoiling the flavour. These yeasts like a temperature of about 65°F. but they do not need yeast nutrients as there are enough present in the wort. The bottom fermenting yeasts do not form a scum since they work from the bottom. They are effective at lower temperatures than top fermenting yeasts and settle down to form a firm sediment.

Preparing the wort for bitter, mild and stout

All equipment should be thoroughly cleaned and sterilised before use as described in Chapter 1, page 9.

You will need for 1 gallon:

Bitter beer

beer yeast made up
   into a starter
4 pints water
pale ale water treatment,
   if necessary
1 oz. Goldings hops ⎱
4 oz. crystal malt ⎰ A

12 oz. malt extract ⎫
12 oz. glucose chips ⎬ B
   or 12 oz. granulated ⎭
   sugar
cooled, boiled water to
   make up to 1 gallon

Mild ale

beer yeast made up into
   a starter
4 pints water
mild ale water treatment,
   if necessary
½ oz. Fuggles hops ⎫
2 oz. crystal malt ⎬ A
2 oz. flaked maize ⎭

6 oz. malt extract ⎱ B
8 oz. granulated sugar ⎰
cooled, boiled water to
   make up to 1 gallon

Stout

stout yeast made up into	8 oz. malt extract
a starter	12 oz. Demerara sugar
4 pints water	cooled, boiled water to
1 teaspoon salt	make up to 1 gallon
2 oz. patent black malt	
½ oz. Fuggles hops	

The ingredients on the left (4 pints water, 1 teaspoon salt, 2 oz. patent black malt, ½ oz. Fuggles hops) are grouped as A. The ingredients on the right (8 oz. malt extract, 12 oz. Demerara sugar, cooled, boiled water to make up to 1 gallon) are grouped as B.

Make up the appropriate yeast into a starter, in accordance with the manufacturer's instructions, (observe precautions set out in Chapter 1, page 7). Measure out the 4 pints water into a saucepan and add the appropriate water treatment or salt. Lightly crack the malt with a rolling pin, taking care not to reduce it to a powder.

Add ingredients A to the water, bring to the boil and simmer for 45 minutes.

Remove from the heat, strain through a nylon sieve. Return the liquid to the rinsed saucepan.

Stand the container of malt extract in a saucepan of warm water until it will pour easily then add ingredients B to the strained liquid; stir thoroughly until dissolved then bring to the boil for a further 10 minutes – no longer. Allow to cool slightly.

Pour into a polythene pail, top up with cooled, boiled water to make up to 1 gallon and allow to cool for about 1 hour, until the temperature is about 65°F. (check with thermometer).

Test the gravity and make a record of the reading.

The wort with fermentation well under way

Preparing the wort for lager

You will need for 1 gallon:

lager yeast made up into	4 pints water
a starter	2 oz. crystal malt
8 oz. sugar	½ oz. hops
¼ teaspoon citric acid	10 oz. malt extract
¼ pint water	
1 teaspoon salt	

The ingredients on the left (8 oz. sugar, ¼ teaspoon citric acid, ¼ pint water) are grouped as A. The ingredients on the right (4 pints water, 2 oz. crystal malt, ½ oz. hops) are grouped as B.

Make up the lager yeast in a starter in accordance with the manufacturer's instructions (observe precautions set out in Chapter 1, page 7). Lightly crack the crystal malt, with a rolling pin, taking care not to reduce it to a powder. Make up a syrup with ingredients A as described in Chapter 1, page 11.

Place the salt and water in a saucepan. Add ingredients B, bring to the boil and simmer for 45 minutes.

Remove from the heat; strain through nylon sieve. Return the liquid to the rinsed saucepan.

Stand the container of malt extract in a saucepan of warm water until it will pour easily.

Add the malt extract and syrup to the strained liquid, stir thoroughly then bring to the boil and boil for a further 10 minutes – no longer. Allow to cool and pour into 1-gallon fermentation jar. Top up to 1-gallon level with cooled, boiled water.

Lightly plug with sterilised cotton wool and when the temperature is 60°F. (test with a thermometer) take a reading of the gravity and record it. Re-plug with cotton wool.

Straining the wort

Pitching with the yeast

Brewers have a language all of their own.
Adding yeast to the wort is called 'pitching with the yeast'.
When the temperature of the wort is about 60°F., add the prepared yeast starter, stirring briskly all the time. Cover the container and put in a warm place.

Fermentation

Bitter, mild or stout The initial fermentation is extremely vigorous. Within a few hours of pitching with the yeast, carbon dioxide bubbles to the surface and shortly afterwards the surface is covered with a froth.
After about a day, remove the froth by skimming it off with a wooden spoon; replace lid.
Then allow to ferment for about 6 days.
Lager As this is a bottom fermenting yeast, no surface scum is formed.
After 2 days, remove cotton wool plug and prepare and fit fermentation lock, as described in Chapter 1, page 11.
Allow to ferment for about 10 days in all.

Racking

Bitter, mild or stout About 5 days after pitching the wort with the yeast, take a gravity reading.
Before racking, you want the gravity of the beer to drop to one-quarter of the reading you made prior to fermentation. Test each day until the gravity reaches the required figure.
When ready for racking, use a siphon as described in Chapter 1, page 13 and rack into a 1-gallon fermentation jar.
Prepare and insert fermentation lock, as described in Chapter 1, page 11 and leave for 7 days.
Lager Again you want the gravity to drop to one-quarter of the original reading before racking.
After about 10 days of fermentation take a reading and rack when the gravity reaches the correct figure.

Priming

A certain amount of unfermented sugar needs to be present prior to bottling so that carbon dioxide will be formed, making the beer sparkling instead of flat. If too much carbon dioxide is present, the beer will be too frothy.
In all probability, the sugar and starchy matter in the must will have all fermented after racking. In this case, the beer has to be primed by the addition of ½ teaspoon sugar to each 1 pint bottle, during bottling. Again, this addition may not be necessary.
The best way of finding out is to use a Clinitest kit which is available from most chemists. This is how you conduct the test.
Mix 5 drops of beer with 10 drops of water in a test tube.
Drop a Clinitest tablet into the test tube and compare the colour, after 30 seconds, with the colour chart provided with the kit.
A bright orange colour indicates that no sugar is present; various shades of green indicate the amount of sugar present.
If bright orange, use 1 teaspoon sugar to each 1 pint of beer.
If colour chart indicates ½% sugar content, this will mean that the equivalent of 1 teaspoon sugar is present in each 1 pint of beer and no sugar needs to be added.
If colour chart indicates more than ½% sugar, allow to ferment longer until permissible amount of sugar is present.

Bottling

Siphon into thoroughly cleaned and sterilised bottles, as described in Chapter 1, page 13.
Fill to within 1-inch of the bottom of the screw-top or the cap.
Add the priming of sugar, if necessary, and tightly secure with screw-top or cap.

Securing the caps with a crown corking machine

Conditioning

Put the bottles in a cool place and leave to condition for 2–3 weeks before drinking.

Pouring

Make sure the glasses are thoroughly clean and dry – free from grease and detergent – before pouring in the beer.

Take care in pouring – do not 'glug' it into the glass. Tilt the glass to the bottle and run the beer slowly and steadily down the side of the glass so that the sediment is not stirred up and so that it can be left behind in the bottle with little wastage. Beers should be served at a temperature of about 50°F., lagers should always be served chilled.

Drinking

All these beers for which recipes have just been given have a high alcoholic content compared with most beers you buy so proceed with caution until you know how much you can take.

Faults that can occur – how to avoid or correct them
Stuck fermentation

1. This can be caused by fermenting the wort at too low a temperature. Move the container to a warmer place – above 60°F. – and stir thoroughly.
2. Stale yeast can be another cause. Make sure you use fresh yeast every time.
3. A badly balanced wort may also cause fermentation to stick. There is no excuse – measure out the quantities accurately.
4. Yeast cells may be inhibited through the presence of hop resins boiled out into solution.

Do not boil the hops for longer than indicated. If you run into trouble, keep the wort well aerated by stirring.

Bitter after-taste

This is called *yeast bite* and can be caused by:-
using too much yeast
fermenting at too high a temperature
not skimming enough
not racking soon enough.

All can be remedied by following instructions correctly.

Hazy beer

This is usually caused by yeast cells floating in suspension and is the result of adding too much yeast. The fault can be remedied by treating with proprietary isinglass beer finings, in accordance with the manufacturer's instructions.

Important points to note

Wash all utensils and equipment as soon as you have finished with them.
Always test the gravity of the wort and keep suitable records.
Make sure you conduct fermentation at a suitable temperature.
Skim the scum off to prevent yeast falling into the beer.
Do not rack until the gravity drops to one-quarter of the original reading.
Do not bottle until you have tested for sugar content.
Store bottles in a cool place to mature.
Serve beer at the correct temperature.
Don't ask a man to drink and drive!

chapter 3
making a white wine from fruit

For the purpose of this exercise, I have chosen apples for making a white wine.
If you have not tasted apple wine, try it first and make sure you like it. It is commercially available from many off-licences in the sweet or dry form. Apple wine is a wine that I much prefer and my

first experience of it was memorable – to say the least. I consumed three pints of it on draught at a tavern, whilst an undergraduate, reeled helplessly afterwards along a towpath and narrowly avoided drowning in the river. So be warned . . . as with so many home-made wines its strength should be treated with respect. Drink it by the wine glass rather than the tumbler.

The best time to make apple wine is when apples are cheap and plentiful – from September onwards. Eating apples do not make good wine. Cider apples are ideal but a mixed variety of cooking apples can be used successfully. Never use russets.

Preparing the fruit

As with all fruit wine recipes, completely sound, ripe fruit should be used, free from blemishes. Just one sub-standard fruit can affect the whole wine. All fruit should be thoroughly washed before use.

Methods of juice extraction

Fruit presses are available (see picture) but at this early stage of your wine-making apprenticeship, I would not advise you to invest in one until you have quite made up your mind to make a lot of home-made wines.

If you are fortunate enough to have an electric domestic juice extractor, this will do admirably. A more laborious but reasonably effective method of juice extraction is to cut the apples into slices, taking care to discard the pips, and crush the slices with the base of a milk bottle.

Boiling is not practised since this destroys a lot of the natural fruit enzymes which break down pectins in the fruit. If these pectins are not broken down they will cause the wine to be hazy. You will then need to resort to the use of pectin-destroying enzymes in quantities that make them anything but cheap. Another aspect of boiling the fruit is that the wine can have a cooked flavour.

Preventing oxidation of the fruit

As you will have noticed, if you cut an apple it quickly becomes brown on the cut surface. This is due to oxidation. To overcome this, sulphite the fruit as quickly as possible with a Campden tablet.

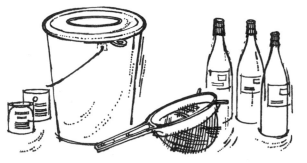

Equipment

You will need all the equipment listed in Chapter 1, page 5, *plus*:

2½-*gallon polythene pail* (mark it to the 1-gallon level, if not indicated) for preparing the must and for initial fermentation.

Nylon sieve for straining the must.

A fruit press

Apple wine (dry)

You will need for 1 gallon:

All-purpose yeast starter	2½ lb. sugar
4 pints water	1 pint water
2 Campden tablets	1 teaspoon citric acid
1 teaspoon pectic enzyme	cooled, boiled water to make up to 1 gallon
12 lb. apples	1 yeast nutrient tablet

Make up a fermentation starter with the yeast, as in Chapter 1, page 7, 2 days before preparing the must.

Clean and sterilise the required equipment, as in Chapter 1, page 9.

Bring the 4 pints water to the boil and allow to cool.

Crush the Campden tablets, dissolve in a little water, and add to the cooled water. Also add the pectic enzyme.

Put the extracted juice or mashed fruit and juice in the cleaned and sterilised pail, and then add the cooled, boiled water. Stir thoroughly and allow to stand overnight.

Make up a syrup with the sugar, water and citric acid as described in Chapter 1, page 11.

Add the syrup to the pail and top up to 1-gallon mark with cooled, boiled water.

Test the gravity and record it.

Add the fermentation starter and yeast nutrient, stir well and replace lid.

Ferment in a warm place for 7 days, stirring or crushing the fruit by hand each day and replacing lid.

After 7 days, strain through a nylon sieve into a cleaned and sterilised fermentation jar.

Prepare and insert fermentation lock, as described in Chapter 1, page 11.

Ferment to a gravity of about 10. Take readings once each week and record them.

When the gravity is around 10 and the wine is beginning to clear, rack as described in Chapter 1, page 13.

Rack a second time before bottling, as described in Chapter 1, page 13.

Note: The wine is ready for drinking after 6 months but improves on keeping for a year.

Apple wine (sweet)

The making of this wine affords a useful exercise in working out syrup additions to give the required sweetness. If you make up a syrup of 2 lb. sugar to 1 pint water, with 1¼ teaspoons citric acid, it will yield 2 pints syrup with a gravity of 300. With this, the required sweetness can be adjusted accordingly.

Follow the recipe and method for making dry apple wine, except add 2 pints cooled, boiled water to the fruit and juice instead of 4 pints to allow for a second addition of syrup. Instead of making up a syrup with 2½ lb. sugar to 1 pint water, make up one with 4 lb. sugar to 2 pints water, with 2 teaspoons citric acid to yield 4 pints of syrup with a gravity of 300. This syrup will be added in two halves – 2 pints at a time.

After adding the first 2 pints syrup, check the gravity of the must and record it. Also check and record the volume.

Then proceed as with the method given for the dry apple wine but do not add the second half of syrup until the wine has fermented to a gravity of about 10.

You can now determine how the second half of syrup should be added to produce a predetermined sweetness.

Suppose for the sake of argument that the original volume of the must was 5 pints and the gravity was 140.

Now supposing you wanted a medium-sweet wine with a gravity of 130 and you want to make 1 gallon.

The required sugar content will be 8 pints × 130 = 1040.

The present sugar content is 5 pints × 140 = 700.

The gravity difference between these two is 1040 − 700 = 340.

The gravity of the syrup is 300.

Quantity of syrup to be added

$$= \frac{\text{gravity difference}}{\text{gravity of syrup}} = \frac{340}{300} = 1.1 \text{ pints} \ldots \text{ or}$$

1 pint, near enough.

Therefore, to produce 8 pints of medium-sweet wine add 1 pint syrup of gravity 300 and 2 pints water to the 5 pints wine.

Supposing you wanted a very sweet wine with a gravity of 160, the required sugar content will be 8 × 160 = 1280. Present sugar content is, as above, 700. And the gravity difference is now 1280 − 700 = 580.

$$\text{Syrup addition} = \frac{\text{gravity difference}}{\text{gravity of syrup}} = \frac{580}{300} =$$

1.9 pints, or 2 pints near enough.

Therefore, to produce 8 pints of very sweet wine, add 2 pints syrup of gravity 300 and 1 pint water to the 5 pints wine.

After adding the second half of syrup and water, refit the fermentation lock and rack when the wine clears.

A very sweet wine will require three rackings and the medium-sweet two before bottling.

Note: These wines can be drunk after a year but they will improve if kept for up to a couple of years.

Important points to note

Always use completely sound fruit and remember to wash it before use.

Always add Campden tablet to the fruit.

Always check the gravity and volume of the must and calculate syrup additions to give the required degree of sweetness.

chapter 4

making a red wine from fruit

This chapter gives details of how to make a red wine with damsons – a wine which is a great favourite in the fruit-growing districts.

Unlike apples, damsons are a soft fruit so you do not have the same problem of juice extraction. But here again, the importance of using sound ripe fruit, free from any kind of defect, cannot be overestimated.

Damsons are extremely rich in pectin and if you were to boil them up, so much pectin would be released that the wine would be almost impossible to clear without very heavy treatment with pectic enzyme. So again, as nearly always, do not boil the fruit and, as an extra precaution some pectic enzyme will be added to keep pectin haze at bay. A Campden tablet is added to the fruit to kill off any micro-organisms.

Damsons are also extremely acid so chalk is added to counteract acidity.

Equipment

You will need all the equipment listed in Chapter 1, page 5, *plus*:

2½-gallon polythene pail for preparing the must and for initial fermentation.

Nylon sieve for straining the must.

Damsons do not make a good dry wine so choose between a medium and a sweet one.

Damson Wine

You will need for 1 gallon:

All-purpose wine yeast starter	½ oz. chalk
3 pints water	1 yeast nutrient tablet
7 lb. damsons	cooled, boiled water
1 teaspoon pectic enzyme	
1 Campden tablet	
4 lb. sugar	
2 pints water	syrup:
2 teaspoons citric acid	gravity 300

Make up a fermentation starter with the yeast, as in Chapter 1, page 7, 2 days before preparing the must.

Clean and sterilise the required equipment, as in Chapter 1, page 9, and measure up the fermentation jar.

Bring the 3 pints water to the boil and allow to cool.

Wash sound fruit and weigh with stones.

Put the fruit into a polythene pail and crush well by hand.

Add the cooled, boiled water, pectic enzyme and Campden tablet, crushed and dissolved in a little water.

Stir well, remove stones and leave covered for 2 hours.

Meanwhile, make up the syrup with the sugar, water and citric acid as described in Chapter 1, page 11. Leave to cool.

Add half the syrup, stir well, check and record the volume and gravity.

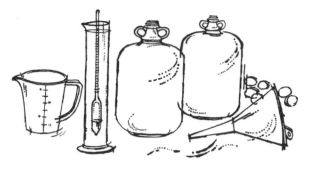

Add the chalk, yeast nutrient tablet and starter. Cover and leave in a warm place for 10 days, stirring each day and then replacing lid.

Gently filter the wine through a nylon sieve into a 1-gallon fermentation jar, taking care not to squeeze the fruit.

Measure the gravity and calculate the amount of syrup that needs to be added to produce a medium or sweet wine – whichever you prefer – using the method described in Chapter 3, page 22. If you cannot be bothered doing this (but go on – make the effort, you are supposed to be learning something) you will need about another 1 pint syrup for the medium and $1\frac{1}{2}$–$1\frac{3}{4}$ pints syrup for the sweet.

In each case, top up to the 1-gallon mark with cooled, boiled water after the syrup addition.

Fit the fermentation lock as described in Chapter 1, page 11, and rack when the wine clears.

Keep the wine in a dark place, through two rackings, to retain its beautiful, dark colour, and bottle when it becomes brilliant.

Note: You can drink the medium wine after about a year. The sweet wine should be kept for at least two years.

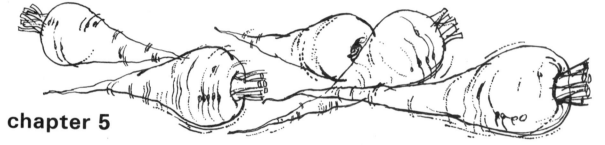

chapter 5

making a wine from root vegetables

This chapter gives details of how to make parsnip wine – a wine which country folk derive a sadistic pleasure in giving to their smart town cousins and seeing them reeling helplessly drunk, as they little suspect its strength.

It is indeed a very 'morish' drink – very acceptable and with little hint through its refreshing flavour of its secret potency. It is a wine which should not be made too dry or too sweet.

When making a wine from root vegetables, they have to be boiled – a process which elsewhere has been avoided. But before doing this they need scrubbing well and the blemishes need cutting out.

January is the best time for parsnips after they have been well-frosted.

As with most root vegetables, parsnips contain a fair amount of starch. If this starch is not converted to sugar, a starch haze could develop in the wine. Starch-destroying enzymes can be used to move this but a more satisfactory way is to starve the yeast of sugar early on so that it has to break the starch down into sugar.

Equipment

You will need all the equipment listed in Chapter 1, page 5, *plus*:

$2\frac{1}{2}$-*gallon polythene pail* for preparing the must and for initial fermentation.

Nylon sieve for straining the must.

24

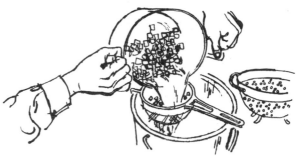

Parsnip wine

You will need for 1 gallon:

All-purpose wine yeast starter
4 lb. parsnips
1 oz. citric acid
4 pints water
8 oz. raisins
3 lb. sugar
1½ pints water
1½ teaspoons citric acid } 3 pints syrup gravity 300

1 yeast nutrient tablet
cooled, boiled water

Make up a fermentation starter with the yeast as in Chapter 1, page 7, 2 days before preparing the must.

Clean and sterilise the required equipment, as in Chapter 1, page 9.

Cut the scrubbed, trimmed parsnips into small cubes and boil gently in 4 pints water with citric acid until they are just soft – not on any account, until they are mushy.

Chop the raisins and put them into the polythene pail.

Strain the parsnip liquor through a nylon sieve on to the chopped raisins.

When thoroughly cooled, measure and record gravity and volume then add the yeast nutrient tablet and starter, stir, cover and allow to ferment for 5 days, stirring and re-covering each day.

Make up the syrup, as described in Chapter 1, page 11.

Strain the liquid and add half of the syrup.

Fit fermentation lock, as described in Chapter 1, page 11, and allow to ferment until the gravity is about 20.

Add the remaining syrup and top up to 1-gallon mark with cooled, boiled water, then replace fermentation lock.

When fermentation ceases, rack as described in Chapter 1, page 13 and rack two more times before bottling.

chapter 6
making a wine from flowers

Flowers have a very distinctive flavour and they can be used to produce some very attractive wines. They are delicately flavoured and are best made into dry, medium dry or medium sweet wines.

Flowers lack acid and sometimes tannin so these need to be added.

Here, instructions are given on how to make a dandelion wine since the flowers are plentiful and the flavour excellent. The method is basically the same for all flower wines, where the flowers are macerated and boiling water is poured over them to extract the flavour.

Gathering the dandelions

Gather the blooms on a sunny day while they are fully open. Pick the heads off the stalks and rinse them in a colander.

Equipment

You will need all the equipment listed in Chapter 1, page 5, *plus*:

1-quart jug for measuring the flowers.
2½-gallon polythene pail for preparing the must and for initial fermentation.
Nylon sieve for straining the must.

Dandelion wine

You will need for 1 gallon:

5 pints water	¼ teaspoon grape tannin
2 quarts dandelions	cooled, boiled water
3 lb. sugar	
1½ teaspoons citric acid	3 pints syrup
1½ pints water	gravity 300
2 lemons	
All-purpose wine yeast starter	
1 yeast nutrient tablet	

Make up a fermentation starter with the yeast as described in Chapter 1, page 7, 2 days before preparing the must.

Clean and sterilise the required equipment, as described in Chapter 1, page 9, and measure up fermentation jar.

Bring the 5 pints water to the boil, put the dandelions in a polythene pail, macerate with a wooden spoon and pour over the boiling water. Cover and leave for 2–3 days – no longer – stirring each day and replacing the cover. Make up the syrup, with the sugar, citric acid and water as described in Chapter 1, page 11,

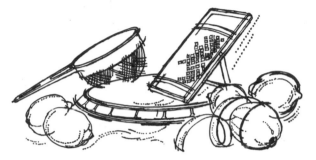

and allow to cool. Strain the must through a nylon sieve into a fresh polythene pail. Add the syrup, finely grated lemon rind, and stir in the lemon juice, yeast starter, nutrient tablet and tannin.

Cover and ferment in a warm place for 7 days. Strain through a nylon sieve into a fermentation jar, top up to 1-gallon mark with cooled, boiled water and fit fermentation lock, as described in Chapter 1, page 11.

Allow to ferment until clear and then rack, as described in Chapter 1, page 13.

Rack again 3 months later and bottle two months after that.

Note: This gives you a dry wine which is ready to drink after about 9 months. For a medium wine, use an extra 8 oz. sugar in the syrup.

chapter 7
making mead

Mead was one of the first alcoholic drinks known to man and it goes right back to the dawn of civilisation. It was much loved by the Vikings and Ancient Britons and was the traditional nuptial celebratory drink, giving birth to the expression 'honeymoon'. The newly-weds would drink it for a whole month after the ceremony – whether this was because it was the only way they

acid must be present to ensure a successful fermentation. $\frac{1}{2}$ oz. citric acid per gallon suffices.

Nutrients Rather more nutrient needs to be added than when making other wines. Add 2 yeast nutrient tablets instead of the usual 1 tablet per gallon, plus Vitamin B_1 in the form of a little Marmite.

Tannin $\frac{1}{4}$ teaspoon tannin is needed to give the mead its required astringency.

could stand the sight of each other is not on record. However, life seems a lot more tolerable after quaffing a few glasses and it is certainly well worth making.

Mead is made by fermenting a solution of honey, and honey, of course, is made by bees from the nectar of flowers.

There are many different kinds of honey available but always remember if you want to make a good mead you must use a good honey. The more common blended honeys that you find in the shops are of little or no use in making mead. Single blossom honeys make the best meads and the most usual, which are available from bee-keepers in this country, are clover honeys. Further afield, orange blossom and acacia honeys are available from Spain and other single blossom honeys come from as far afield as Mexico, Guatemala and Australia.

The honey may be in a liquid or crystalline state but this has no bearing on the quality of the mead. If you are going to use canned honey, you will find it more economical to buy it in bulk from a home wine supplier's shop. Tinned honey is a sterilised product but if you are going to buy honey from an apiarist, it will need sterilising first with a Campden tablet.

Equipment

You will need the same equipment as used in Chapter 1, page 5.

Dry mead

You will need for 1 gallon:

All-purpose wine yeast starter	$\frac{1}{4}$ teaspoon Marmite
4 pints water	$\frac{1}{4}$ teaspoon grape tannin
pinch Epsom salts	3 lb. white honey
$\frac{1}{2}$ oz. citric acid	1 Campden tablet
2 yeast nutrient tablets	cooled, boiled water

Make up a fermentation starter with the yeast as in Chapter 1, page 7, 2 days before preparing the must, and mark the 1-gallon level of the fermentation jar.

Clean and sterilise the required equipment as in Chapter 1, page 9.

Bring the 4 pints water to the boil and allow to cool.

When cool add the Epsom salts, acid, nutrient tablets, Marmite, tannin and honey. Stir until dissolved.

Add Campden tablet, crushed and dissolved in a little water.

Pour into the fermentation jar and top up to the 1-gallon mark with cooled, boiled water.

Bung and allow to stand for 24 hours.

Add fermentation starter, fit the fermentation lock, as in Chapter 1, page 11, and put the jar in a warm place.

After about 10 days, fill the jar to the neck with cooled, boiled water and replace fermentation lock.

Allow to ferment to a gravity of about 15 and then rack, as described in Chapter 1, page 13. When the gravity drops to 0, bottle the wine as described in Chapter 1, page 13.

Note: Mature for at least a year before drinking.

Additions to the must

Trace elements If there are no magnesium salts in your water supply, add a pinch of Epsom salts. This will help prevent the fermentation from sticking.

Acid As with the making of all wines, sufficient

Sweet mead

The ingredients are exactly the same as with Dry Mead except that 4 lb. honey are used instead of 3 lb.

A Sauternes yeast starter can be used instead of the All-purpose one.

Proceed as with the Dry Mead but rack when the gravity is just below 20 and again when it is below 15. It will be ready for bottling after about six months.

These are just two of the many kinds of meads that can be made. Other recipes, including those for metheglin, melomel and pyment – there are some medieval names to conjure with – are given under MEAD RECIPES, page 53.

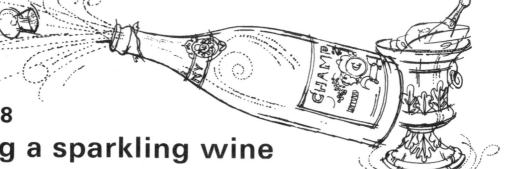

chapter 8
making a sparkling wine

The best way to make a sparkling wine is by design and not by accident. If you bottle your wines inadvertently before fermentation is completely finished you might well get the bottle exploding.

Which brings us to the first point: when making a sparkling wine you need to use strong Champagne bottles and special corks.

Sparkling wines are not the easiest of wines to make and need quite a lot of practice. And it is best to make sure you understand and master the principles of making an ordinary still wine before making a sparkling wine. For sparkling wines are made from ordinary still wines which are subsequently treated to give them their special characteristics. However, you start off by using a Champagne yeast to enhance the sparkling qualities of the wine.

A little syrup and Champagne yeast is introduced to the still wine in the Champagne bottle before it is corked and sealed. Plastic corks and wires are available from your home wine equipment stockist which makes corking and sealing quite easy.

The resulting sediment from renewed fermentation can be removed by complicated freezing methods but these hardly seem worth the trouble when one realises how cheaply sparkling wines can be made and that most of the wine can be served, leaving behind a small portion which is unusable because of the sediment.

Almost any wine can be rendered sparkling but there are only a few which are worth the trouble of making in this fashion.

These are dealt with in Chapter 15, page 56.

Here we will concern ourselves with the 'Champagnisation' of an apple wine.

Equipment

You will need all the equipment listed in Chapter 1, page 5, *plus*:

$2\frac{1}{2}$-*gallon polythene pail* for preparing the must and for initial fermentation.

Nylon sieve for straining the must.

Champagne bottles, plastic corks and wires.

Sparkling apple wine

Use the recipe and method for sweet or dry wine, as in Chapter 3, page 22, substituting a Champagne yeast starter for the All-purpose yeast starter.

When the wine is clear and stable, after about 6 months, siphon into Champagne bottles, making sure that they are absolutely clean and sterile. Leave a 1-inch space at the neck.

To each bottle, add 2 teaspoons syrup, gravity 300 (see page 22) and a few drops of Champagne yeast starter.

Fit the corks in place and wire them down.

Keep the bottles at a temperature of 65°F. for the first 14 days.

Then move to a temperature of 50°F. to store so that further yeast activity is slowed down.

Store at this temperature for 6 months to a year before drinking.

Serving

Chill the wine and have the glasses ready before opening the bottle. Pour steadily into glasses with a smooth action so that all the wine is served, leaving the sediment in the bottle without clouding the wine which is poured out.

If you are not serving wine to a large number of people who can drink all the wine use a half bottle.

Make sure you have enough glasses ready to take all the clear contents of the bottle in one pouring.

There will be enough sparkle in the wine for it to be retained in the glass by the time your guests are ready for a second helping.

chapter 9
making a sherry

Sherry is an oxidised wine – a wine which needs to be fermented in the presence of air to produce its characteristic flavour. A special sherry yeast is the other requirement and the wine is finished off by fortifying with spirit.

Dry sherry ideally requires the formation of a sherry flor film on the wine while it is fermenting and to achieve this a starting gravity of *exactly* 116 is required.

After fermentation both dry and sweet sherries need aerating as they are racked from their deposit. This is done by splashing the wine about while siphoning so that air is bubbled in.

A sweet sherry needs a starting gravity in the region of 160.

When you make sherries, they are going to improve considerably with ageing so those who are impatient should stick to wines which are drinkable when young.

Plums, prunes, grape concentrate, dates, parsnips and raisins lend themselves to making sherries. Here we will concern ourselves with making a sherry from raisins. Other recipes for making sherries are given in Chapter 18, page 66.

Equipment

You will need all the equipment listed in Chapter 1, page 5, excluding the fermentation lock, *plus*: *Nylon sieve* for straining the must.

Dry sherry

You will need for 1 gallon:

5 lb. raisins, chopped	1 yeast nutrient
4 pints boiling water	tablet
syrup, gravity 300	sherry yeast starter
1 Campden tablet	¾ pint 80° proof spirit

Boil the raisins with the water for 5 minutes.

Cover and leave to stand for 24 hours.

Press and strain through a nylon sieve into a 1-gallon fermentation jar.

Test the gravity of the must and calculate the amount of syrup and water to be added to produce a gallon of must with a gravity of 116 (see pages 22, 67).

After the correct additions have been made,

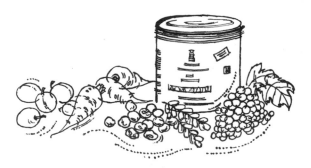

add the yeast nutrient and starter, shake well, and lightly plug with cotton wool.

When fermentation has finished, siphon the wine from its deposit, aerating the wine as much as possible, into a clean fermentation jar.

Lightly plug with cotton wool and rack again with plenty of aeration.

If the wine tastes too dry for your taste, sweeten with grape concentrate.

Before bottling, fortify with $\frac{3}{4}$ pint 80° proof spirit and mix well (or fortify to taste, as described on page 67).

Note: Allow to mature in the bottle for 2 years.

Sweet sherry

Proceed as with making dry sherry but add enough syrup to make up 1 gallon must to a gravity of 160 (see pages 22, 67).

chapter 10

how to consult and use the wine recipes

Quite apart from flavour, the thing that most people are concerned about is whether a wine is too sweet or too dry.

You, as the home wine-maker, can make a wine as dry or as sweet as you like. Remember, this is wholly determined by the starting gravity of the must, providing satisfactory fermentation is carried out. So I would strongly advise you to find out what starting gravity of the must produces a wine which satisfies your palate to the required degree of dryness or sweetness.

You will notice that the vast majority of these recipes use sugar made up into a syrup with a gravity of 300. As has been previously stated this is a very convenient form of sugar addition and is one which makes calculations simpler. It may be that you might prefer more syrup or less syrup than indicated in the individual recipes and by using the hydrometer as your yardstick and the calculations as described on pages 8, 67 you can achieve the required gravity. Remember, too, that the sugar content of fruit and vegetables can vary considerably depending on what kind of summer there has been – if any – and when they are picked. Again, the hydrometer tells you exactly what the score is. Perhaps a starting gravity of 95 for the must produces the required degree of dryness for your taste. In which case, work out the exact syrup addition to achieve this figure. Or perhaps you like your wines really sweet with a gravity of 155 – again you may need more syrup than indicated in the recipe. Strength of flavour is another factor on which some people have strong ideas. The fruit wines, in particular, can have a very strong flavour which is not agreeable to all tastes. You may find that you want to cut down on the quantity of fruit and there is no reason at all why you should not do so.

Experiment, experiment, experiment . . . this is the keynote to successful wine-making – making wines that please *you*. So use the recipes as a guide and then go on to prove you can make better wines than anyone else.

Ingredients In addition to fresh produce for making wines, as and when it is in season, there is a whole range of canned and dried produce which enable you to make wines throughout the year. Do not scorn the supermarket shelf in the long dark days of winter – there is scope here for making excellent wines.

Blending You may find that having made a wine it is not to your taste. And you might think you have had a lot of trouble for nothing. But providing the wine is sound, it can be made good use of. Try blending it with other wines with a more pronounced or a less pronounced flavour, as required, and you may well produce a very attractive wine. Many a commercial wine owes its success to the skill of the blender.

Which wines should you make? The first determining factor is one of economics. If you live in the country, there is a wide range of produce growing free and for the picking. If you have a garden of any size and you grow fruit and vegetables, these are an obvious choice for your first wine-making efforts. Perhaps you have a birch tree nearby. Tap it and have a drink off it! It makes a delicious wine.

Finding your way through the sections Wines are arranged in alphabetical order under the sections Dry White, Sweet White, Rosé, Sparkling, Dry Red, Sweet Red, Ports, Sherries and Mead Wines. This enables you to turn to recipes in a category of wine that appeals to your palate without wading through a whole list of wines that do not interest you.

chapter 11
dry white wines

Home wine-makers who prefer dry wines to sweet have a decided advantage – dry wines can all be drunk within a year and sometimes after only six months.

Yet dry wines are not all that predictable; depending on what you make them from, they have their good years and bad years. The quality of the raw materials is a big determining factor.

Tannin and acid content of the fruit may vary, and the correct proportions are needed to produce a really first class wine.

It is always advisable to serve dry white wines chilled – but not ice cold.

Apple wine
(Using canned apple juice)

You will need for 1 gallon:

19-oz. can apple juice	1 yeast nutrient
2–2½ pints syrup,	tablet
gravity 300	All-purpose wine yeast
cooled, boiled water	starter

Make up directly into fermentation jar.

Test the gravity of the juice and adjust the sugar and water additions to give the required starting gravity of the must.

Fit fermentation lock and ferment to completion in a warm place.

Rack and mature in the usual way.

Apricot wine

You will need for 1 gallon:

6 lb. fresh apricots
4 oz. sultanas
4 pints boiling water
1 Campden tablet
2 teaspoons pectic
 enzyme
2 pints syrup, gravity
 300

1 yeast nutrient
 tablet
All-purpose wine yeast
 starter
cooled, boiled water

Remove the stones from the apricots and cut up the flesh. Chop the sultanas.

Put the apricots and sultanas in a polythene pail, pour over the boiling water and stir.

When cool, add the Campden tablet, crushed and dissolved in a little water, and the pectic enzyme. Cover and leave for 3 days, stirring each day.

Add the 2 pints syrup, yeast nutrient tablet and starter, and stir.

Cover and leave to ferment in a warm place for 7 days, stirring each day and then replacing lid.

Press and strain through nylon sieve into a 1-gallon fermentation jar, top up with cooled, boiled water to 1-gallon mark and fit fermentation lock.

When fermentation is completed, move the wine to a cool place.

Rack, bung and bottle in the usual way.

Note: Keep for at least a year before drinking.

Apricot wine

(Using canned apricots)

You will need for 1 gallon:

15-oz. can apricots
4 pints cooled,
 boiled water
2¼ pints syrup,
 gravity 300
1 teaspoon citric acid
3 teaspoons pectic
 enzyme

½ teaspoon grape
 tannin
1 yeast nutrient
 tablet
Sauternes yeast starter
cooled, boiled water

Mash the fruit and put the syrup in the fermentation jar.

Put the mashed fruit in a polythene pail, add the water, syrup, citric acid, pectic enzyme and grape tannin.

Mix well, cover and allow to stand for 3 days, crushing the fruit by hand each day and then recovering.

Press and strain into a 1-gallon fermentation jar, add the yeast nutrient tablet and starter; top up to the 1-gallon mark with cooled, boiled water; fit fermentation lock.

Ferment to completion in a warm place.

Rack and mature in the usual way.

Apricot and raisin wine

You will need for 1 gallon:

2 lb. fresh apricots
1 lb. raisins
4 pints boiling water
1 Campden tablet
1 teaspoon pectic
 enzyme
2 pints syrup,
 gravity 300

1 yeast nutrient
 tablet
All-purpose wine
 yeast starter
cooled, boiled water

Remove the stones from the apricots and chop the fruit. Chop the raisins.

Put the apricots and raisins in a polythene pail, pour over the boiling water and stir.

When cool, add the Campden tablet, crushed and dissolved in a little water, and the pectic enzyme. Cover and leave for 3 days, stirring each day.

Add the 2 pints syrup, yeast nutrient tablet and starter, and stir.

Cover and leave to ferment in a warm place for 7 days, stirring each day and then replacing lid.

Press and strain through nylon sieve into a 1-gallon fermentation jar, top up to 1-gallon mark with cooled, boiled water and fit fermentation lock.

When fermentation is completed, move the wine to a cool place.

Rack, bung and bottle in the usual way.

Note: May be drunk after 6 months.

Birch sap wine

You will need for 1 gallon:

6 pints birch sap
2½ lb. sugar
grated rind 2 lemons
12 oz. raisins
juice 2 lemons

1 yeast nutrient
 tablet
All-purpose wine
 yeast starter
cooled, boiled water

The time to tap off the birch sap is in March while it is rising. Do this by making a hole about a foot from the ground, insert a piece of polythene tubing trailing into a jar to collect the sap. It will take a few days to collect the sap. Afterwards, plug the hole with a piece of cork. Under no circumstances tap a tree of less than 6-inches in diameter or you will kill the tree.

When you have collected the birch sap, bring it to the boil with the sugar, lemon rind and chopped raisins, and simmer for 10 minutes.

When cool, transfer to a polythene pail, add the lemon juice, yeast nutrient tablet and starter.

Cover and allow to ferment for 4 days, stirring each day and then replacing lid.

Strain into a 1-gallon fermentation jar, top up with cooled, boiled water and fit fermentation lock.

Ferment to completion in a warm place.
Rack and mature in the usual way.

Bramble tip wine

You will need for 1 gallon:

4 lb. young blackberry tips
1 lb. raisins
5 pints boiling water
2¼ pints syrup, gravity 300
1 teaspoon citric acid
1 yeast nutrient tablet
Bordeaux yeast starter
cooled, boiled water

Chop the bramble tips and boil them in the water for 30 minutes.
Chop the raisins and put them in a polythene pail.
Strain on the bramble liquor and stir well.
When cool, add the syrup, citric acid, yeast nutrient tablet and starter. Stir well.
Cover and ferment for 4 days in a warm place, stirring each day and then replacing lid.
Transfer to 1-gallon fermentation jar and top up to 1-gallon mark with cooled, boiled water before fitting fermentation lock.
When fermentation is completed, move the wine to a cool place.
Rack, bung and bottle in the usual way.
Note: Keep for a year before drinking.

Broad bean wine

You will need for 1 gallon:

1 lemon
4 lb. shelled old broad beans
5 pints water
4 oz. sultanas
2½ pints syrup, gravity 300
juice 1 lemon
1 yeast nutrient tablet
All-purpose wine yeast starter
cooled, boiled water

Peel the lemon rind thinly and put with the beans in the water and simmer 1 hour.
Strain the liquid through a nylon sieve on to the sultanas and syrup in a polythene pail.
When cool, stir in the lemon juice, yeast nutrient tablet and yeast starter.
Allow to ferment for 10 days in a warm place, stirring each day and then replacing lid.
Strain into a 1-gallon fermentation jar, top up to 1-gallon mark with cooled, boiled water and fit fermentation lock.
Ferment to dryness and rack, bung and bottle in the usual way.

Broom wine

You will need for 1 gallon:

2 pints petals, lightly pressed down
5 pints boiling water
2¼ pints syrup, gravity 300
2 lemons
¼ teaspoon grape tannin
1 yeast nutrient tablet
All-purpose wine yeast starter
cooled, boiled water

Wash the petals in a colander and put into a polythene pail.
Pour over 5 pints boiling water, cover and leave for 3 days, stirring each day and then replacing lid.
Strain through a nylon sieve into a second polythene pail, add syrup, finely grated lemon rind, lemon juice, grape tannin, yeast nutrient tablet and starter.
Strain again a week later into a 1-gallon fermentation jar, top up to 1-gallon level with cooled, boiled water and fit fermentation lock.
Rack twice at 3-monthly intervals and then bottle.

Celery wine

You will need for 1 gallon:

4 lb. celery sticks
1 orange
1 lemon
5 pints water
2¼ pints syrup, gravity 300
1 yeast nutrient tablet
Chablis yeast starter
cooled, boiled water

Clean the celery and chop into small dice, peel the orange and lemon rinds thinly and place in a saucepan with the water and celery. Bring to the boil and cook until the celery is tender.
Strain the liquid on to the syrup in a polythene pail.
When cool, add the orange and lemon juice, yeast nutrient tablet and starter.
Allow to ferment for 10 days in a warm place, stirring each day and then replacing lid.
Strain into a 1-gallon fermentation jar, top up to 1-gallon mark with cooled, boiled water and fit fermentation lock.
Ferment to dryness and rack, bung and bottle in the usual way.

Clover wine

Follow the recipe for Broom Wine, page 33, substituting clover for the broom petals.
Remove the green button from the base of the flowers.

Coltsfoot wine

Follow the recipe for Broom Wine, page 33, substituting coltsfoot for the broom petals.
Remove the green button from the base of the flowers.

Cowslip wine

Follow the recipe for Broom Wine, page 33, substituting cowslips for the broom petals.

Date wine

You will need for 1 gallon:

8 oz. flaked barley	1 yeast nutrient
7 pints water	tablet
2 lb. dates	sherry yeast starter
1 oz. citric acid	cooled, boiled water

Boil the flaked barley in the 7 pints water for 15 minutes.
Strain through a sieve, add chopped dates and citric acid; boil for 10 minutes.
Strain through a sieve into a polythene pail and, when cool, add yeast nutrient tablet and starter.
Cover and ferment for 4 days in a warm place, stirring each day and then replacing lid.
Pour into a 1-gallon fermentation jar, leaving behind as much of the sediment as possible, top up to 1-gallon mark with cooled, boiled water and fit fermentation lock.
Rack when the wine begins to clear and then move it to a cool place.
When clear, and fermentation is completed, rack into bottles.

Elderflower wine

Follow the recipe for Broom Wine, page 33, substituting elderflowers for broom petals.
Wait until the flowers just begin to fall. Then rub the flowers from the heads into a bowl. This way the petals fall and the heads can be discarded.

Gooseberry wine

You will need for 1 gallon:

3 lb. hard, green gooseberries	2½ pints syrup, gravity 300
5 pints boiling water	1 yeast nutrient tablet
1 Campden tablet	Chablis yeast starter
1 teaspoon pectic enzyme	cooled, boiled water

Top and tail the gooseberries and wash well.
Place in a polythene pail and pour over the boiling water.
When cool, crush the gooseberries by hand.
Add Campden tablet, crushed and dissolved in a little water, and the pectic enzyme.
Leave covered for 3 days, crushing the fruit by hand each day.
Stir in the syrup, yeast nutrient tablet and starter.
Cover and ferment for 7 days, stirring each day and then replacing lid.
Press and strain through a nylon sieve into 1-gallon fermentation jar, and top up to 1-gallon mark with cooled, boiled water before fitting fermentation lock.
When fermentation is completed, move the wine to a cool place.
Rack, bung and bottle in the usual way.
Note: Allow 1–2 years for the wine to mature.

Gorse wine

Follow recipe for Broom Wine, page 33, substituting gorse for the broom petals.

Grapefruit wine

You will need for 1 gallon:

juice 6 large, ripe grapefruit	1 yeast nutrient tablet
grated rind 1 grapefruit	All-purpose wine yeast starter
5 pints cooled, boiled water	2½ pints syrup, gravity 300
1 teaspoon pectic enzyme	1 Campden tablet cooled, boiled water

Put the juice and grated peel into a polythene pail.
Add the rest of the ingredients – excluding the syrup – and the Campden tablet, crushed and dissolved in a little water.
Stir well and leave to ferment in a warm place for 3 days, stirring each day and then replacing lid.
Strain into a 1-gallon fermentation jar, add the syrup, top up to the 1-gallon mark with cooled, boiled water and fit fermentation lock.
Ferment to completion in a warm place.
Rack and mature in the usual way.

Grapefruit wine

(Using canned grapefruit juice)

You will need for 1 gallon:

19-oz. can grapefruit juice	1 yeast nutrient tablet
2–2½ pints syrup, gravity 300	All-purpose wine yeast starter
½ teaspoon grape tannin	cooled, boiled water

Make up directly into fermentation jar.
Test the gravity of the juice and adjust the sugar and water additions to give the required starting gravity of the must.
Fit fermentation lock and ferment to completion in a warm place.
Rack and mature in the usual way.

Great burnet wine

Follow recipe for Broom Wine, page 33, substituting great burnets for the broom petals.

Greengage wine

You will need for 1 gallon:

4 lb. greengages	1 yeast nutrient tablet
4 pints cooled, boiled water	All-purpose wine yeast starter
1 Campden tablet	cooled, boiled water
2½ pints syrup, gravity 300	

Wash and cut up sound fruit and put in a polythene pail.
Add the cooled, boiled water plus a Campden tablet crushed and dissolved in a little water. Leave for about 1 hour.
Stir in 1½ pints of the syrup, yeast nutrient tablet and starter.
Cover and leave to ferment in a warm place for 10 days, breaking the fruit up by hand each day and then replacing lid.
Strain through a nylon sieve into a 1-gallon fermentation jar, add the remaining syrup and top up to 1-gallon mark with cooled, boiled water before fitting fermentation lock.
Move the wine to a cool place when fermentation is finished and bung.
Rack when clear and again 2–3 months later. Siphon into bottles.
Note: May be drunk after six months.

Guava wine

(Using canned guavas)

You will need for 1 gallon:

3 14-oz. cans guavas	3 teaspoons pectic enzyme
4 pints cooled, boiled water	1 teaspoon grape tannin
2¼ pints syrup, gravity 300	1 yeast nutrient tablet
3 teaspoons citric acid	All-purpose wine yeast starter

Follow the method set out for Apricot Wine (using canned apricots) page 32.

Hawthorn wine

Follow recipe for Broom Wine, page 33, substituting hawthorn for the broom petals.

Hawthorn berry wine

Follow the recipe for Rosehip Wine, page 38, substituting hawthorn berries for rosehips.

Honeysuckle wine

Follow recipe for Broom Wine, page 33, substituting honeysuckle for the broom petals.

Mango wine

(Using canned mangoes)

You will need for 1 gallon:

16-oz. can mango slices
4 pints cooled,
  boiled water
2¼ pints syrup,
  gravity 300
3 teaspoons citric
  acid
3 teaspoons pectic
  enzyme
1 teaspoon grape tannin
1 yeast nutrient
  tablet
All-purpose wine
  yeast starter

Follow the method set out for Apricot Wine (using canned apricots) page 32.

Marigold wine

Follow the recipe for Broom Wine, page 33, substituting marigolds for the broom petals. Remove the green button from the base of the flowers.

Orange wine

You will need for 1 gallon:

6 Seville oranges
6 sweet oranges
4 oz. raisins
4 pints cooled,
  boiled water
2 pints syrup,
  gravity 300
1 Campden tablet
1 yeast nutrient
  tablet
Chablis yeast starter
cooled, boiled water

Slice the unpeeled oranges, chop the raisins and put in a polythene pail.
Add the cooled, boiled water, syrup, Campden tablet crushed and dissolved in a little water, yeast nutrient tablet and starter.
Cover and ferment in a warm place for 7 days, crushing the fruit by hand each day and then replacing lid.
Strain through a nylon sieve into a second polythene pail, cover and allow to ferment for another 3 days.
Pour into a 1-gallon fermentation jar, leaving behind as much of the sediment as possible, and top up to 1-gallon mark with cooled, boiled water before fitting fermentation lock.

Move to a cooler place, ferment until clear and then rack.
Rack again after three months and then siphon off into bottles.
Note: This wine is ready to drink after about a year.

Pansy wine

Follow recipe for Broom Wine, page 33, substituting pansies for the broom petals.

Parsley wine

You will need for 1 gallon:

1 lb. fresh parsley
  leaves
2 lemons
5 pints water
4 oz. raisins, chopped
2½ pints syrup,
  gravity 300
1 yeast nutrient tablet
Chablis yeast starter
cooled, boiled water

Boil the parsley and thinly peeled lemon rind in 5 pints water for 20 minutes.
Stir in the chopped raisins and syrup.
When cool, stir in the lemon juice, yeast nutrient tablet and yeast starter.
Transfer to a 1-gallon fermentation jar, top up to 1-gallon mark with cooled, boiled water and fit fermentation lock.
Rack when the wine begins to clear and again before bottling.

Pea pod wine

You will need for 1 gallon:

4 lb. young pea pods
1 lemon
5 pints water
2½ pints syrup,
  gravity 300
4 oz. sultanas
1 yeast nutrient
  tablet
Chablis yeast starter
cooled, boiled water

Boil the young pea pods and thinly peeled lemon rind in the water until the pods are tender.
Strain on to the syrup and sultanas in a polythene pail.
When cool, add the lemon juice, yeast nutrient tablet and starter.
Cover and allow to ferment in a warm place for 5 days, stirring each day and replacing lid.
Strain into a 1-gallon fermentation jar, top up to 1-gallon mark with cooled, boiled water and fit fermentation lock.
Rack and mature for 9 months.
Note: Best drunk young.

Peach wine

You will need for 1 gallon:

3 lb. peaches
4 pints cooled, boiled water
½ oz. pectic enzyme
2 pints syrup, gravity 300
1 teaspoon citric acid
½ teaspoon tannin
1 yeast nutrient tablet
All-purpose wine yeast starter
cooled, boiled water

Remove stones from peaches, chop up the flesh and put into a polythene pail.

Add cooled, boiled water, mash the peaches by hand and leave covered overnight.

Stir in pectic enzyme and leave for 2 days.

Strain through a nylon sieve into a second polythene pail.

Add the syrup, citric acid, tannin, yeast nutrient tablet and starter.

Cover and ferment for 7 days in a warm place, stirring each day and replacing lid.

Pour into 1-gallon fermentation jar, leaving behind as much sediment as possible, top up to 1-gallon mark with cooled, boiled water before fitting fermentation lock.

Ferment to completion in a warm place and then bung.

Put into a cool place to clear and then rack.

Siphon into bottles.

Note: Drinkable after 6 months.

Pear wine

You will need for 1 gallon:

1 lb. raisins, chopped
1 pint boiling water
6 lb. dessert pears
4 pints cooled, boiled water
1 Campden tablet
1 teaspoon pectic enzyme
2 pints syrup, gravity 300
1 yeast nutrient tablet
All-purpose wine yeast starter
cooled, boiled water

Boil the raisins in the 1 pint water for 5 minutes and allow to cool.

Wash and crush the pears in a polythene pail, add the raisins (plus liquid) and the 4 pints water, Campden tablet, crushed and dissolved in a little water, and the pectic enzyme.

Allow to stand for 24 hours, squeeze through a muslin bag and transfer the liquid to a 1-gallon fermentation jar.

Add the syrup, yeast nutrient tablet and starter; top up to 1-gallon mark with cooled, boiled water and fit fermentation lock.

Ferment to completion in a warm place.

Rack and mature in the usual way.

Pineapple wine

(Using canned pineapple juice)

You will need for 1 gallon:

1–1½ pints pineapple juice per gallon wine
2–2½ pints syrup, gravity 300
1 teaspoon citric acid
½ teaspoon grape tannin
1 yeast nutrient tablet
All-purpose wine yeast starter
cooled, boiled water

Make up directly into fermentation jar. Test the gravity of the juice and adjust the sugar and water additions to give the required starting gravity of the must.

Fit fermentation lock and ferment to completion in a warm place. Rack and mature.

Primrose wine

Follow recipe for Broom Wine, page 33, substituting primroses for the broom petals.

Rhubarb wine

You will need for 1 gallon:

4 lb. ripe rhubarb
6 oz. raisins, chopped
5 pints boiling water
1 Campden tablet
1 teaspoon pectic enzyme
1 lemon
2¼ pints syrup, gravity 300
1 yeast nutrient tablet
All-purpose wine yeast starter
cooled, boiled water

Use red, fully ripe, non-forced rhubarb. Trim off the leaves and roots, wash well and chop. Bruise with a rolling pin, put into a polythene pail with the raisins and pour on the boiling water.

Allow to cool, then add the Campden tablet, crushed and dissolved in a little water, the pectic enzyme and thinly peeled lemon rind.

Cover and leave for 4 days, stirring each day and pulping the rhubarb, and then replacing lid.

Strain and press into a 1-gallon fermentation jar, add the syrup, yeast nutrient tablet and starter; top up to the 1-gallon mark with cooled, boiled water and fit fermentation lock.

Ferment to completion in a warm place.

Rack and mature in the usual way.

Rosehip wine

You will need for 1 gallon:

2 lb. rosehips
2 lemons
5 pints boiling water
1 Campden tablet
1 teaspoon pectic
  enzyme
2¼ pints syrup,
  gravity 300

1 yeast nutrient
  tablet
All-purpose yeast
  starter
cooled, boiled water

Wash the rosehips in a colander and then crush them, taking care not to crush the pips.

Put the crushed rosehips in a polythene pail, add the thinly peeled lemon rind and then pour on boiling water.

When cool, add a Campden tablet, crushed and dissolved in a little water, the pectic enzyme, lemon juice, syrup, yeast nutrient tablet and starter.

Allow to ferment for 10 days in a warm place, stirring each day and then replacing lid.

Press and strain through a nylon sieve into a 1-gallon fermentation jar, top up with cooled, boiled water and fit fermentation lock.

Ferment to completion in a warm place.

Rack and mature in the usual way.

Vine wine

You will need for 1 gallon:

1 gallon vine leaves
  and shoots
5 pints cooled,
  boiled water
2 Campden tablets
juice 1 lemon
1 teaspoon pectic
  enzyme

2¼ pints syrup,
  gravity 300
1 yeast nutrient
  tablet
All-purpose wine
  yeast starter
cooled, boiled water

Collect the leaves and shoots in June before they start to fruit.

Place in a colander and wash well under running water, put into a polythene pail and bruise well with the base of a milk bottle.

Pour on the cooled, boiled water and add the Campden tablets, crushed and dissolved in a little water.

Stir in the lemon juice and pectic enzyme, cover and allow to stand for 3 days, stirring each day and then replacing lid.

Press and strain into a 1-gallon fermentation jar, add the syrup, yeast nutrient tablet and starter, top up to 1-gallon mark with cooled, boiled water and fit fermentation lock.

Ferment to completion in a warm place.

Rack and mature in the usual way.

White currant wine

You will need for 1 gallon:

2 Campden tablets
2 pints cooled,
  boiled water
4 lb. white currants
1 teaspoon pectic
  enzyme

2¼ pints syrup,
  gravity 300
1 yeast nutrient tablet
All-purpose wine
  yeast starter
cooled, boiled water

Dissolve the Campden tablets in the 2 pints water. Add the white currants and crush well by hand. Cover and leave for 2 days, re-crushing each day. Strain through a nylon sieve into a 1-gallon fermentation jar, add the syrup, yeast nutrient tablet and starter; top up to 1-gallon level with cooled, boiled water and fit fermentation lock. Ferment to completion in a warm place.

Rack and mature in the usual way.

chapter 12

sweet white wines

Yes, you have to wait longer for your wines to mature if you like them sweet. Here, the balance is not so critical as with dry white wines; the sweetness can cover any slight blemishes.

Always make sure you add your syrup in two separate lots as indicated in the recipes. Too much syrup at the start of fermentation will inhibit the yeast and the wine may not develop to its full strength.

Care should also be taken with the racking. Make sure you rack off all remaining yeast cells so that the wine remains stable.

Almond wine

You will need for 1 gallon:

2 oz. almonds, (mostly sweet with a few bitter added)
1 lb. raisins
5 pints water
thinly peeled rind 2 lemons
juice 2 lemons
3 pints syrup, gravity 300
1 yeast nutrient tablet
Sauternes yeast starter
cooled, boiled water

Chop the almonds and raisins and simmer in the water, together with the lemon rind, for 30 minutes.

When cool, strain into a 1-gallon fermentation jar, add the lemon juice, half the syrup, the yeast nutrient tablet and starter.

Fit fermentation lock and ferment for 5 days. Add the remaining syrup, top up with cooled, boiled water, refit fermentation lock.

Ferment to completion in a warm place.

Rack and mature in the usual way.

Apricot wine

(Using canned apricots)

You will need for 1 gallon:

1 lb. 12-oz. can apricots
4 pints cooled, boiled water
3 pints syrup, gravity 300
1 teaspoon citric acid
3 teaspoons pectic enzyme
½ teaspoon grape tannin
1 yeast nutrient tablet
Sauternes yeast starter
cooled, boiled water

Mash the fruit and put the syrup in the fermentation jar.

Put the mashed up fruit in a polythene bucket, add the water, half the syrup, citric acid and pectic enzyme and grape tannin.

Mix well, cover and allow to stand for 3 days, crushing the fruit by hand each day and then re-covering.

Press and strain into a 1-gallon fermentation jar, add the yeast nutrient tablet and starter, and fit fermentation lock.

After 7 days, add the remaining syrup, top up to 1-gallon mark with cooled, boiled water and refit fermentation lock.

Ferment to completion in a warm place.

Rack and mature in the usual way.

Apricot and raisin wine

You will need for 1 gallon:

4 lb. fresh apricots
1 lb. raisins
4 pints boiling water
1 Campden tablet
2 teaspoons pectic enzyme
3 pints syrup, gravity 300
1 yeast nutrient tablet
Sauternes yeast starter
cooled, boiled water

Remove the stones from the apricots and cut up the flesh. Chop the raisins.

Put the apricots and raisins in a polythene pail, pour over the boiling water and stir.

When cool, add the Campden tablet, crushed and dissolved in a little water, and the pectic enzyme.

Cover and leave for 3 days, stirring each day.

Add half the syrup, the yeast nutrient tablet and starter, and stir.

Cover and leave to ferment in a warm place for 7 days, stirring each day and then replacing lid.

Press and strain through nylon sieve into 1-gallon fermentation jar, add the remaining syrup and top up to 1-gallon mark with cooled, boiled water before fitting fermentation lock.

When fermentation is completed, move the wine to a cool place.

Rack, bung and bottle in the usual way.

Note: Keep for at least a year before drinking.

Banana wine

You will need for 1 gallon:

4 lb. peeled, over-ripe bananas
8 oz. banana skins
thinly peeled rind 1 lemon and 1 orange
4 pints water
3 pints syrup, gravity 300
juice 1 lemon and 1 orange
1 yeast nutrient tablet
All-purpose wine yeast starter
cooled, boiled water
4 oz. raisins, chopped

Simmer the peeled bananas, banana skins and the orange and lemon rind in the water for 30 minutes.

Press and strain through nylon sieve into a polythene pail.

Stir in half the syrup.

When cool, add the orange and lemon juice, yeast nutrient tablet and starter.

Cover and ferment in a warm place for 7 days, stirring each day and then replacing lid.

Pour into a 1-gallon fermentation jar, add the remaining syrup, top up with cooled, boiled water, and fit fermentation lock.

After a week, move the wine to a cooler place and

leave for another 6 weeks, during which time a thick sediment will form.

Siphon off into a second fermentation jar, add chopped raisins and fit fermentation lock.

Rack two more times at 2-monthly intervals then bottle.

Note: This wine improves with age.

Spiced banana wine

You will need for 1 gallon:

4 lb. peeled, over-ripe bananas	½ oz. citric acid
8 oz. banana skins	1 teaspoon grape tannin
1 oz. cloves	1 yeast nutrient tablet
1 oz. root ginger	All-purpose wine
4 pints boiling water	yeast starter
3½ pints syrup, gravity 300	cooled, boiled water

Thinly slice the bananas and skins into a polythene pail and add cloves and ginger.

Pour on the boiling water and stir.

When cool, add 2 pints of the syrup, the citric acid, grape tannin, yeast nutrient tablet and starter.

Cover and ferment in a warm place for 10 days, stirring each day and then replacing lid.

Press and strain through nylon sieve into a 1-gallon fermentation jar, add the remaining syrup, top up to 1-gallon mark with cooled, boiled water and fit fermentation lock.

Rack twice at 2-monthly intervals and then bottle.

Note: This wine also improves with age.

Banana and parsnip wine

You will need to make 1 gallon:

5 lb. parsnips	½ oz. citric acid
4 pints water	½ teaspoon grape tannin
2 lb. bananas, including skins	1 yeast nutrient tablet
3½ pints syrup, gravity 300	All-purpose wine yeast starter
	cooled, boiled water

Scrub the parsnips, slice thinly and cook in the 4 pints water until just tender – do not over-cook.

Thinly slice the bananas and skins into a polythene pail.

Add the water in which the parsnips were boiled and 2 pints of the syrup.

When cool, add citric acid, grape tannin, yeast nutrient and starter.

Cover and ferment in a warm place for 10 days, stirring each day and then replacing lid.

Press and strain through nylon sieve into a 1-gallon fermentation jar.

Add the remaining syrup, top up to 1-gallon mark with cooled, boiled water and fit fermentation lock.

Rack twice at 2-monthly intervals and then bottle.

Banana and prune wine

You will need for 1 gallon:

2 lb. bananas, including skins	½ teaspoon grape tannin
2 lb. prunes	1 yeast nutrient tablet
4 pints boiling water	All-purpose wine
8 oz. raisins, chopped	yeast starter
3 pints syrup, gravity 300	cooled, boiled water
½ oz. citric acid	

Thinly slice the bananas, skins and prunes into a polythene pail.

Pour in the boiling water, add the chopped raisins and half the syrup.

When cool, add the citric acid, grape tannin, yeast nutrient tablet and starter.

Cover and ferment in a warm place for 10 days, stirring each day and then replacing lid.

Press and strain through nylon sieve into a 1-gallon fermentation jar.

Add the remaining syrup, top up to 1-gallon mark with cooled, boiled water and fit fermentation lock

Rack twice at 2-monthly intervals and then bottle.

Banana and rice wine

You will need for 1 gallon:

2 lb. bananas, including skins	½ teaspoon grape tannin
3 lb. long grain rice	1 yeast nutrient tablet
8 oz. stoned raisins	All-purpose wine
4 pints boiling water	yeast starter
3½ pints syrup, gravity 300	cooled, boiled water
½ oz. citric acid	

Finely chop the bananas and skins, and put into a polythene pail, together with the rice and raisins.

Pour on the boiling water.

When cool, add 2 pints of the syrup, the citric acid, grape tannin, yeast nutrient tablet and starter.

Cover and ferment in a warm place for 10 days, stirring each day and then replacing lid.

Press and strain through nylon sieve into a 1-gallon fermentation jar.

Add the remaining syrup, top up to 1-gallon

mark with cooled, boiled water and fit fermentation lock.

Rack twice at 2-monthly intervals and then bottle.

Barley wine

You will need for 1 gallon:

3 lb. crushed barley
1 lb. potatoes
2 lb. raisins
5 pints boiling water
2½ pints syrup,
   gravity 300
1 Campden tablet

½ teaspoon pectic
   enzyme
1 yeast nutrient
   tablet
All-purpose wine
   yeast starter
cooled, boiled water

Wash the barley, clean and dice the potatoes, chop the raisins and put into a polythene pail. Pour over the boiling water.

When cool, add 2 pints of the syrup, the Campden tablet, crushed and dissolved in a little water, pectic enzyme, yeast nutrient tablet and starter.

Cover and allow to ferment in a warm place for 3 weeks.

Strain into a 1-gallon fermentation jar, add the remaining syrup, top up to the 1-gallon mark with cooled, boiled water and fit fermentation lock.

Ferment to completion in a warm place.

Rack and mature in the usual way.

Broom wine

You will need for 1 gallon:

2 pints petals,
   lightly pressed down
5 pints boiling water
2¾ pints syrup,
   gravity 300
grated rind and juice
   2 lemons

¼ teaspoon grape
   tannin
1 yeast nutrient
   tablet
All-purpose yeast
   starter
cooled, boiled water

Wash the petals in a colander and put into a polythene pail.

Pour over the boiling water, cover and leave for 3 days, stirring each day and replacing lid.

Strain through a nylon sieve into a second polythene pail, add 2 pints of the syrup, finely grated lemon rind, lemon juice, grape tannin, yeast nutrient tablet and starter.

Strain again a week later into a 1-gallon fermentation jar, add the remaining syrup, top up to 1-gallon level with cooled, boiled water and fit fermentation lock.

Rack twice at 3-monthly intervals and then bottle.

Caraway and gooseberry wine

You will need for 1 gallon:

1 oz. caraway seeds
1 lb. flaked barley
4 pints boiling water
2 lb. gooseberries
3 pints syrup,
   gravity 300
1 teaspoon citric acid

¼ teaspoon grape
   tannin
1 yeast nutrient
   tablet
All-purpose wine
   yeast starter
cooled, boiled water

Put the caraway seeds and flaked barley in a polythene pail and pour over the boiling water.

Mash the gooseberries and stir in together with half the syrup.

Stir in the citric acid, tannin, yeast nutrient tablet and starter.

Cover and ferment in a warm place for 10 days, stirring each day and replacing lid.

Strain through a nylon sieve into a 1-gallon fermentation jar, add the remaining syrup and top up to 1-gallon mark with cooled, boiled water before fitting fermentation lock.

When fermentation has finished, rack and move the wine to a cool place.

Mature and bottle in the usual way.

Note: Ready for drinking after a year.

Carrot wine

You will need for 1 gallon:

4 lb. carrots
5 pints water
¼ oz. pectic enzyme
1 Campden tablet
3¾ pints syrup,
   gravity 300

All-purpose wine
   yeast starter
1 yeast nutrient
   tablet
cooled, boiled water

Scrub the carrots and slice thinly.

Put the sliced carrots into the water, bring to the boil and simmer until tender.

When cool, strain the liquid into a 1-gallon fermentation jar, add the pectic enzyme and Campden tablet, crushed and dissolved in a little water, and 2 pints of the syrup.

Allow to stand for 24 hours.

Stir in the remaining syrup, yeast starter and nutrient

tablet; top up to the 1-gallon mark with cooled, boiled water and fit fermentation lock.
Ferment to completion in a warm place and then bung.
Put into a cool place to clear and then rack.
Siphon into bottles after about 6 months.

Cherry plum wine

You will need for 1 gallon:

5 lb. cherry plums
8 oz. raisins, chopped
thinly peeled rind
  2 lemons
4 pints boiling water
juice 2 lemons
1 teaspoon pectic
  enzyme

1 Campden tablet
1 yeast nutrient
  tablet
Sauternes yeast starter
3 pints syrup,
  gravity 300
cooled, boiled water

Remove the stalks and wash the cherry plums. Mash them in a polythene pail and add the chopped raisins and lemon rind. Pour on the boiling water.
When cool, mash the fruit again and add lemon juice, pectic enzyme and Campden tablet, crushed and dissolved in a little water.
Allow to stand for 24 hours.
Add the yeast nutrient tablet, starter and half the syrup, stir well and cover.
Allow to ferment for 6 days in a warm place, stirring each day and then replacing lid.
Strain into a 1-gallon fermentation jar, add the remaining syrup, top up to the 1-gallon mark with cooled, boiled water and fit fermentation lock.
Ferment to completion in a warm place and then bung.
Put into a cool place to clear and then rack.
Siphon into bottles after about six months.

Clover wine

Follow the recipe for Broom Wine, page 41, substituting clover for the broom petals.
Remove the green button from the base of the flowers.

Coffee wine

You will need for 1 gallon:

8 oz. ground coffee
grated rind 2 lemons
4 pints water
8 oz. sultanas
juice 2 lemons
3 pints syrup,
  gravity 300

1 yeast nutrient
  tablet
All-purpose wine
  yeast starter
cooled, boiled water

Simmer the coffee and grated rind in water for 30 minutes.

Strain the liquid on to the chopped sultanas in a polythene pail.
When cool, add the lemon juice, half the syrup, the yeast nutrient tablet and starter.
Allow to ferment for 7 days in a warm place, stirring each day and then replacing lid.
Strain into a 1-gallon fermentation jar, add the remaining syrup, top up to the 1-gallon mark with cooled, boiled water and fit fermentation lock.
Ferment to completion in a warm place and then bung.
Put into a cool place to clear and then rack.
Siphon into bottles after about six months.

Coltsfoot wine

Follow the recipe for Broom Wine, page 41, substituting coltsfoot for the broom petals. Remove the green button from the base of the flowers.

Cowslip wine

Follow recipe for Broom Wine, page 41, substituting cowslips for the broom petals.

Crab apple wine

You will need for 1 gallon:

10 lb. ripe crab apples
4 pints cooled,
  boiled water
1 yeast nutrient
  tablet
All-purpose wine
  yeast starter

1 teaspoon pectic
  enzyme
2 Campden tablets
3 pints syrup,
  gravity 300
1 lb. raisins, chopped
cooled, boiled water

Wash the crab apples, chop and then crush them. Put them in a polythene pail, add the cooled, boiled water, the yeast nutrient tablet and the starter, pectic enzyme and Campden tablets, crushed and dissolved in a little water.
Cover and leave to ferment in a warm place for 7 days, stirring and mashing the apples each day and then replacing lid.
Stir and then strain into a second polythene pail and add half the syrup and the chopped raisins.
Cover and leave to ferment in a warm place for another 14 days.
Strain into a fermentation jar, add the remaining syrup, top up to 1-gallon mark with cooled, boiled water and fit fermentation lock.
When clear and there is a firm sediment, rack off into a second jar and refit fermentation lock.
Rack again 3 months later into bottles.

Date wine

You will need for 1 gallon:

2 lb. dates	4 pints water
thinly peeled rind and juice 1 lemon	3 pints syrup, gravity 300
thinly peeled rind and juice 1 orange	1 yeast nutrient tablet
thinly peeled rind and juice 1 grapefruit	All-purpose wine yeast starter
8 oz. flaked barley	cooled, boiled water

Chop the dates and put in a saucepan with the rinds and fruit juice.
Boil the flaked barley in the water for 15 minutes.
Strain through a nylon sieve on to the dates and fruit.
Boil for 10 minutes.
Strain through a sieve into a polythene pail and, when cool, add half the syrup, the yeast nutrient tablet and starter.
Cover and ferment in a warm place for 4 days, stirring each day and then replacing lid.
Pour into a 1-gallon jar, leaving behind as much sediment as possible, add the remaining syrup, top up to 1-gallon mark with cooled, boiled water and fit fermentation lock.
Rack when the wine begins to clear and then move it to a cool place.
When clear and fermentation is completed rack into bottles.

Elderflower wine

Follow the recipe for Broom Wine, page 41, substituting elderflowers for the broom petals.
Wait until the flowers just begin to fall. Then rub the flowers from the heads into a bowl. This way the petals fall and the heads can be discarded.

Fig wine

You will need for 1 gallon:

2½ lb. dried figs	1 yeast nutrient tablet
4½ pints water	Sauternes yeast starter
3 pints syrup, gravity 300	cooled, boiled water
juice 2 lemons	

Soak the figs overnight in ½ pint of the water.
Add the remaining water, bring to the boil and simmer for 20 minutes.
Stir in half the syrup.
Pour into a polythene pail and, when cool, add lemon juice, yeast nutrient tablet and starter.
Leave covered to ferment in a warm place for 7 days, stirring each day and then replacing lid.
Press and strain into 1-gallon fermentation jar,

add remaining syrup, top up to 1-gallon mark with cooled, boiled water and fit fermentation lock.
Rack when the wine clears after about 3 months. Rack again after another 3 months and then bottle.

Fruit salad wine

(Using canned fruit)

You will need for 1 gallon:

1 lb. 12-oz. can fruit salad	1 teaspoon grape tannin
4 pints cooled, boiled water	3 pints syrup, gravity 300
2 teaspoons citric acid	1 yeast nutrient tablet
3 teaspoons pectic enzyme	Sauternes yeast starter

Follow the recipe for Apricot Wine (using canned apricots) page 39.

Ginger wine

You will need for 1 gallon:

3 oz. root ginger	3 pints syrup, gravity 300
4 pints water	1 yeast nutrient tablet
thinly peeled rind 2 lemons and 2 oranges	All-purpose wine yeast starter
12 oz. raisins, chopped	cooled, boiled water
juice 2 oranges and 2 lemons	

Crush the root ginger and boil in the water, together with the fruit rinds for 30 minutes.
Pour into a polythene pail and add the chopped raisins, fruit juice and half the syrup.
When cool, add the yeast nutrient tablet and starter.
Allow to ferment for 10 days in a warm place, stirring each day and then replacing lid.
Strain into a 1-gallon fermentation jar, add the remaining syrup, top up to the 1-gallon mark with cooled, boiled water and fit fermentation lock.
Ferment to completion in a warm place and then bung.
Put into a cool place to clear and then rack.
Siphon into bottles when clear.

Gooseberry wine

You will need for 1 gallon:

6 lb. ripe green gooseberries
4 pints boiling water
1 Campden tablet
2 teaspoons pectic enzyme
3 pints syrup, gravity 300
1 yeast nutrient tablet
All-purpose wine yeast starter
cooled, boiled water

Top and tail the gooseberries and wash well.
Place in a polythene pail and pour over the boiling water.
When cool, crush the gooseberries by hand.
Add Campden tablet, crushed and dissolved in a little water, and the pectic enzyme.
Leave covered for 3 days, crushing the fruit by hand each day.
Stir in half the syrup, yeast nutrient tablet and starter.
Cover and ferment for 7 days, stirring each day and then replacing lid.
Press and strain through a nylon sieve into a 1-gallon fermentation jar, add the remaining syrup and top up with cooled, boiled water to 1-gallon mark before fitting fermentation lock.
When fermentation is completed, move the wine to a cool place.
Rack, bung and bottle in the usual way.
Note: This wine is ready for drinking after a year.

Gorse wine

Follow recipe for Broom Wine, page 41, substituting gorse for the broom petals.

Great burnet wine

Follow recipe for Broom Wine, page 41, substituting great burnets for the broom petals.

Greengage wine

You will need for 1 gallon:

5 lb. greengages
4 pints cooled, boiled water
1 Campden tablet
3 pints syrup, gravity 300
1 yeast nutrient tablet
All-purpose wine yeast starter
cooled, boiled water

Wash and chop the fruit, discarding the stones, and put in a polythene pail.
Add the cooled, boiled water plus the Campden tablet, crushed and dissolved in a little water.
Leave for about 1 hour.

Stir in half the syrup, the yeast nutrient tablet and starter.
Cover and leave to ferment in a warm place for 10 days, breaking up the fruit by hand each day and then replacing lid.
Strain through a nylon sieve into a 1-gallon fermentation jar, add the remaining syrup, and top up to 1-gallon mark with cooled, boiled water before fitting fermentation lock.
Move the wine to a cool place when fermentation is completed and bung.
Rack when clear and again 2–3 months later.
Siphon into bottles.
Note: Keep for at least a year before drinking.

Hawthorn wine

Follow recipe for Broom Wine, page 41, substituting hawthorn for the broom petals.

Hawthorn berry wine

You will need for 1 gallon:

$\frac{3}{4}$ gallon hawthorn berries
thinly peeled rind 2 oranges
4 oz. raisins, chopped
4 pints boiling water
1 teaspoon pectic enzyme
1 Campden tablet
juice 2 oranges
3 pints syrup, gravity 300
1 yeast nutrient tablet
Sauternes yeast starter
cooled, boiled water

Wash the berries and put in a polythene pail, together with the orange rind and chopped raisins. Pour over the boiling water.
When cool, crush the berries by hand, add the pectic enzyme, Campden tablet, crushed and dissolved in a little water, and the orange juice.
Cover and leave to stand for a day.
Stir in half the syrup, the yeast nutrient tablet and starter, cover and leave to ferment for 5 days in a warm place, stirring each day and then replacing lid.
Strain through a nylon sieve into a 1-gallon fermentation jar, add the remaining syrup, top up with cooled, boiled water and fit fermentation lock.
Ferment to completion in a warm place.
Rack and mature in the usual way.

Honeysuckle wine

Follow recipe for Broom Wine, page 41, substituting honeysuckle for the broom petals.

Kohlrabi wine

You will need for 1 gallon:

4 lb. kohlrabi	1 teaspoon pectic
5 pints water	enzyme
2 lb. sugar	1 yeast nutrient
1 orange, sliced	tablet
3 pints syrup,	All-purpose wine
gravity 300	yeast starter
1 Campden tablet	cooled, boiled water

Scrub the kohlrabi and then cut into thin slices. Boil in the water until tender.

Strain the liquid on to sugar in a second saucepan and add the orange slices. Simmer for 30 minutes. When cool, strain into 1-gallon fermentation jar, add half the syrup, the Campden tablet, crushed and dissolved in a little water, pectic enzyme, yeast nutrient and starter, and fit fermentation lock.

Allow to ferment for 7 days in a warm place, add the remaining syrup top up to the 1-gallon mark with cooled, boiled water and refit fermentation lock.

Rack after 3 months and refit fermentation lock. Rack again after a further 3 months into bottles.

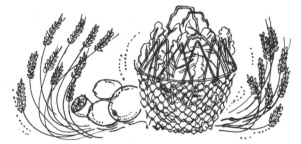

Lettuce wine

You will need for 1 gallon:

3 lb. lettuce	1 Campden tablet
1 lb. wheat	3 pints syrup,
thinly peeled rind	gravity 300
1 orange and 1 lemon	1 yeast nutrient
5 pints water	tablet
juice 1 orange and	All-purpose wine
1 lemon	yeast starter
8 oz. raisins, chopped	cooled, boiled water
$\frac{1}{4}$ oz. pectic enzyme	

Wash and chop lettuce; discard the stalks. Put in a saucepan with the wheat, rinds and water, bring to the boil and simmer for 15 minutes.

Strain into a polythene pail and, when cool, stir in the fruit juice, chopped raisins, pectic enzyme and Campden tablet, crushed and dissolved in a little water.

Allow to stand for 24 hours.

Add the yeast nutrient tablet, starter and half the syrup, stir well and cover.

Allow to ferment for 7 days in warm place, stirring each day and then replacing lid.

Strain into a 1-gallon fermentation jar, add the remaining syrup, top up to the 1-gallon mark with cooled, boiled water and then fit the fermentation lock.

Ferment to completion in a warm place and then bung.

Siphon into bottles after about 6 months.

Lychee wine

(Using canned lychees)

You will need for 1 gallon:

1 lb. 4-oz. can lychees	$\frac{1}{2}$ teaspoon grape
4 pints cooled,	tannin
boiled water	1 yeast nutrient
3 pints syrup,	tablet
gravity 300	All-purpose wine
1 teaspoon citric acid	yeast starter
3 teaspoons pectic	
enzyme	

Follow the recipe for Apricot Wine (using canned apricots) page 39.

Maize wine

You will need for 1 gallon:

1 lb. crushed maize	juice 2 lemons
1 pint water	$3\frac{1}{2}$ pints syrup,
thinly peeled rind	gravity 300
2 lemons	1 yeast nutrient tablet
1 lb. raisins, chopped	Tokay yeast starter
4 pints boiling water	cooled, boiled water

Wash the maize and soak overnight in the 1 pint water.

Pour into a polythene pail and add the lemon rind and raisins and pour over the boiling water.

When cool, add the lemon juice, 2 pints of the syrup, yeast nutrient tablet and starter.

Cover and leave to ferment in a warm place for 7 days, stirring each day and then replacing lid.

Strain into 1-gallon fermentation jar, add the remaining syrup, top up with cooled, boiled water and fit fermentation lock.

Rack when clear and move the wine to a cool place.

Rack again, three months later, into bottles.

Marigold wine

Follow the recipe for Broom Wine, page 41, substituting marigolds for the broom petals. Remove the green button from the base of the flowers.

Marrow wine

You will need for 1 gallon:

4 lb. ripe marrows
4 pints water
1 Campden tablet
thinly peeled rind and
    juice 1 lemon
thinly peeled rind and
    juice 2 oranges
¼ oz. pectic enzyme

1 yeast nutrient
    tablet
All-purpose wine
    yeast starter
3½ pints syrup,
    gravity 300
cooled, boiled water

Slice the marrow pulp into a polythene pail. Pour over the water and add the Campden tablet, crushed and dissolved in a little water. Add the rind and juice of the citrus fruit and the pectic enzyme.
Cover and allow to stand for 24 hours.
Add the yeast nutrient tablet, starter and 2 pints of the syrup, stir well and cover.
Allow to ferment for 7 days in a warm place, stirring each day and then replacing lid.
Strain into a 1-gallon fermentation jar, add the remaining syrup, top up to the 1-gallon mark with cooled, boiled water and fit fermentation lock.
Ferment to completion in a warm place and then bung.
Put into a cool place to clear and then rack.
Siphon into bottles after about six months.

Medlar wine

You will need for 1 gallon:

8 lb. medlars
1 lb. raisins, chopped
5 pints boiling water
1 Campden tablet
1 teaspoon pectic
    enzyme

1 yeast nutrient
    tablet
Sauternes yeast starter
2½ pints syrup,
    gravity 300
cooled, boiled water

Store the medlars until they are fully ripe. Wash and then crush them in a polythene pail, add the chopped raisins and pour on the boiling water.
When cool, stir in the Campden tablet, crushed and dissolved in a little water, and the pectic enzyme.
Leave to stand overnight then add yeast nutrient tablet and starter, cover, and ferment in a warm place for 7 days, stirring each day and then replacing lid.
Strain without pressing through a nylon sieve into a 1-gallon fermentation jar, add 1½ pints of the syrup and fit fermentation lock.
Ferment for 7 days then add the remaining syrup, top up to 1-gallon mark with cooled, boiled water and refit fermentation lock.
Ferment to completion in a warm place.
Rack and mature in the usual way.

Mint wine

You will need for 1 gallon

1½ pints mint leaves
3½ pints syrup,
    gravity 300
4 pints boiling water
¼ teaspoon grape
    tannin

1 teaspoon citric acid
1 yeast nutrient
    tablet
All-purpose wine
    yeast starter
cooled, boiled water

Chop the mint and put into a polythene pail.
Add 2 pints of the syrup and pour on the boiling water. Add the grape tannin and citric acid.
When cool, stir in the yeast nutrient tablet and starter.
Cover and ferment in a warm place for 10 days, stirring each day and then replacing lid.
Strain into a 1-gallon fermentation jar, add the remaining syrup, top up to 1-gallon mark with cooled, boiled water and fit fermentation lock.
Ferment to completion in a warm place.
Rack and mature in the usual way.

Oak bud wine

You will need for 1 gallon:

8 oz. oak buds
1 lb. raisins, chopped
4 pints water
4 pints syrup,
  gravity 300
1 Campden tablet
juice 1 lemon
1 yeast nutrient
  tablet
All-purpose wine
  yeast starter
cooled, boiled water

Pick the buds just after the first leaves open. Put them in a saucepan with the chopped raisins and water and simmer for 30 minutes.
Strain into a polythene pail and stir in half the syrup.
When cool add the Campden tablet, crushed and dissolved in a little water, lemon juice, yeast nutrient tablet and starter.
Cover and allow to ferment in a warm place for 7 days, stirring each day and then replacing lid.
Strain into a 1-gallon fermentation jar, add the remaining syrup, top up with cooled, boiled water and fit fermentation lock.
Ferment to completion in a warm place.
Rack and mature in the usual way.

Orange wine

You will need for 1 gallon:

12 sweet oranges
1 lb. raisins
3 pints cooled,
  boiled water
3½ pints syrup,
  gravity 300
1 Campden tablet
1 yeast nutrient
  tablet
Sauternes yeast starter
cooled, boiled water

Slice the oranges with their peel, chop the raisins and put, with the oranges, into a polythene pail.
Add the cooled, boiled water, 2 pints of the syrup, Campden tablet crushed and dissolved in a little water, yeast nutrient tablet and starter.
Cover and ferment in a warm place for 7 days, crushing the fruit by hand each day and then replacing lid.
Strain into a second polythene pail, cover and allow to ferment for another 3 days.
Pour into a 1-gallon fermentation jar, leaving behind as much of the sediment as possible, add the remaining syrup and top up to 1-gallon mark with cooled, boiled water before fitting fermentation lock.
Move the wine to a cool place, ferment until clear and then rack.
Rack again after 3 months and then siphon off into bottles.
Note: Ready to drink after a year; improves with keeping for up to 3 years.

Pansy wine

Follow the recipe for Broom Wine, page 41, substituting pansies for the broom petals.

Paw paw wine

(Using canned paw paws)

You will need for 1 gallon:

2 16-oz. cans paw paws
4 pints cooled,
  boiled water
2 teaspoons citric acid
½ teaspoon tannin
3 pints syrup,
  gravity 300
1 yeast nutrient
  tablet
All-purpose wine
  yeast starter
cooled, boiled water

Follow the method for Apricot Wine (using canned fruit) page 39.

Peach wine

You will need for 1 gallon:

3 lb. peaches
4 pints cooled,
  boiled water
½ oz. pectic enzyme
3 pints syrup,
  gravity 300
1 teaspoon citric acid
½ teaspoon grape
  tannin
1 yeast nutrient tablet
Tokay yeast starter
cooled, boiled water

Remove stones from peaches, chop the flesh and put in a polythene pail.
Add cooled, boiled water, mash the peaches by hand and leave covered overnight.
Stir in pectic enzyme and leave for 2 days.
Strain through a nylon sieve into a second polythene pail.
Add 2 pints of the syrup, citric acid, tannin, yeast nutrient tablet and starter.
Cover and ferment for 7 days in a warm place, stirring each day and replacing lid.
Pour into 1-gallon fermentation jar, leaving behind as much sediment as possible, add the remaining syrup and top up to 1-gallon mark with

cooled, boiled water, before fitting fermentation lock.
Ferment to completion in a warm place and then bung.
Put in a cool place to clear and then rack.
Siphon into bottles.
Note: Drinkable after a year; better after 2 years.

Pineapple wine

(Using canned pineapples)

You will need for 1 gallon:

2 15-oz. cans pineapple chunks	3 pints syrup, gravity 300
4 pints cooled, boiled water	1 yeast nutrient tablet
2 teaspoons citric acid	All-purpose wine yeast starter
½ teaspoon grape tannin	cooled, boiled water

Chop the pineapple finely, put in a polythene pail with the 4 pints cooled, boiled water, citric acid, grape tannin, half the syrup, yeast nutrient tablet and starter. Mix thoroughly and ferment for 10 days, stirring and mashing the fruit by hand each day and then replacing lid.
Sieve into a 1-gallon fermentation jar, add the remaining syrup (plus the syrup from the can), top up with cooled, boiled water and fit fermentation lock.
Ferment to completion in a warm place.
Rack and mature in the usual way.

Potato wine

You will need for 1 gallon:

5 lb. potatoes	juice 2 lemons
4 pints water	1 yeast nutrient tablet
4 pints syrup, gravity 300	All-purpose wine yeast starter
thinly peeled rind 2 lemons	cooled, boiled water

Use small, old potatoes. Scrub them well, quarter and simmer in the water for about 20 minutes, until just tender but not mushy.
Strain the liquid into a second saucepan, add half the syrup and the lemon rind and simmer for 15 minutes.
When cool, strain into a 1-gallon fermentation jar, add the fruit juice, yeast nutrient tablet and starter, and fit fermentation lock.
Ferment for 10 days in a warm place, then add the remaining syrup, top up to 1-gallon mark with

cooled, boiled water and refit fermentation lock.
Ferment to completion in a warm place.
Rack and mature in the usual way.

Potato and raisin wine

You will need for 1 gallon:

1 lb. potatoes	1 yeast nutrient tablet
2 lb. raisins, chopped	All-purpose wine yeast starter
1 lb. wheat	juice 2 lemons
4 pints water	cooled, boiled water
3 pints syrup, gravity 300	

Scrub the potatoes, quarter and put into a polythene pail with the chopped raisins and wheat.
Bring the water and half the syrup to the boil, then pour into the polythene pail.
When cool, add the yeast nutrient tablet, starter, and the lemon juice, stir, cover and allow to ferment in a warm place for 3 weeks.
Strain into a 1-gallon fermentation jar, add the remaining syrup, top up to the 1-gallon mark with cooled, boiled water and fit fermentation lock.
Ferment to completion in a warm place.
Rack and mature in the usual way.

Primrose wine

Follow recipe for Broom Wine, page 41, substituting primroses for the broom petals.

Pumpkin wine

You will need for 1 gallon:

6 lb. pumpkin	1 yeast nutrient tablet
2 oranges, sliced	Sauternes yeast starter
2 lemons, sliced	3½ pints syrup, gravity 300
4 pints boiling water	cooled, boiled water
1 Campden tablet	

Chop the pumpkin flesh and place in a polythene pail with the oranges and lemons.
Pour on the boiling water, cover and allow to stand overnight.
Add the Campden tablet, crushed and dissolved in a little water, the yeast nutrient tablet and starter.
Cover and allow to ferment for 4 days, stirring each day and then replacing lid.
Add half the syrup, stir, cover and allow to ferment for another 7 days.
Strain into a 1-gallon fermentation jar, add the remaining syrup, top up to the 1-gallon mark

with cooled, boiled water and fit fermentation lock.

Rack, when clear, and move the wine to a cool place.

Rack again, 3 months later, into bottles.

Note: Ready for drinking after 6 months.

Quince wine

You will need for 1 gallon:

4 lb. quinces	2¾ pints syrup,
1 lb. raisins, chopped	gravity 300
5 pints hot water	1 yeast nutrient
1 Campden tablet	tablet
1 teaspoon pectic	Sauternes yeast starter
enzyme	cooled, boiled water

Wash, slice and mash ripe quinces into a polythene pail. Add the chopped raisins then pour on the hot water.

When cool, add the Campden tablet, crushed and dissolved in a little water and the pectic enzyme.

Cover and allow to stand for 3 days.

Strain into a 1-gallon fermentation jar, add 1½ pints of the syrup, yeast nutrient tablet and starter, and fit fermentation lock.

Allow to ferment for 7 days in a warm place, add the remaining syrup, top up to the 1-gallon mark with cooled, boiled water and refit fermentation lock.

Ferment to completion in a warm place.

Rack and mature in the usual way.

Rhubarb wine

You will need for 1 gallon:

4 lb. rhubarb	3 pints syrup,
6 pints boiling water	gravity 300
1 Campden tablet	1 yeast nutrient
1 teaspoon pectic	tablet
enzyme	Sauternes yeast starter
thinly peeled rind	cooled, boiled water
1 lemon	

Use red, fully ripe, non-forced rhubarb. Trim off the leaves and roots, wash well and chop.

Bruise with a rolling pin, put into polythene pail and pour on the boiling water.

Allow to cool then add the Campden tablet, crushed and dissolved in a little water, the pectic enzyme and lemon rind.

Cover and leave for 4 days, stirring each day and then replacing lid.

Strain and press into 1-gallon fermentation jar, add half the syrup, yeast nutrient tablet and starter and fit fermentation lock.

Allow to ferment for 10 days in a warm place and then add the remaining syrup, top up to 1-gallon mark with cooled, boiled water and refit fermentation lock.

Ferment to completion in a warm place.

Rack and mature in the usual way.

Rice wine

You will need for 1 gallon:

3 lb. long grain rice	1 yeast nutrient
1 lb. raisins	tablet
5 pints boiling water	All-purpose wine
1 Campden tablet	yeast starter
3 pints syrup,	cooled, boiled water
gravity 300	

Crush the rice, chop the raisins and put them both in a polythene pail.

Pour on the boiling water.

When cool, add the Campden tablet, crushed and dissolved in a little water, half the syrup, the yeast nutrient tablet and starter.

Cover and allow to ferment in a warm place for 3 weeks.

Strain into a 1-gallon fermentation jar, add the remaining syrup, top up to the 1-gallon mark with cooled, boiled water and fit fermentation lock.

Ferment to completion in a warm place.

Rack and mature in the usual way.

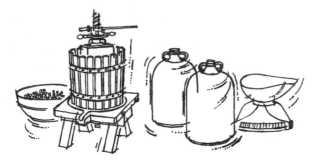

Rosehip wine

You will need for 1 gallon:

3½ lb. rosehips
4 pints water
8 oz. raisins
thinly peeled rind
   2 lemons
1 Campden tablet
1 teaspoon pectic
   enzyme

juice 2 lemons
3 pints syrup,
   gravity 300
1 yeast nutrient
   tablet
Tokay yeast starter
cooled, boiled water

Wash the rosehips in a colander and then crush them, taking care not to crush the pips.

Put the crushed rosehips in a polythene pail, add the raisins and lemon rind and then pour on boiling water.

When cool, add the Campden tablet, crushed and dissolved in a little water, the lemon juice, pectic enzyme, half the syrup, yeast nutrient tablet and starter.

Allow to ferment for 10 days in a warm place, stirring each day and then replacing lid.

Press and strain through a nylon sieve into a 1-gallon fermentation jar, add the remaining syrup, top up to the 1-gallon mark with cooled, boiled water and fit fermentation lock.

Ferment to completion in a warm place.

Rack when it clears after about 3 months and move to a cool place.

Leave for a further 3 months before bottling.
Note: Ready to drink after a year.

Dried rosehip wine

You will need for 1 gallon:

12 oz. dried rosehips
1 pint water
thinly peeled rind
   1 lemon
4 pints water
8 oz. raisins, chopped
1 Campden tablet
1 teaspoon pectic
   enzyme

juice 1 lemon
3 pints syrup,
   gravity 300
1 yeast nutrient
   tablet
cooled, boiled water

Soak the rosehips overnight in the 1 pint water. Then pour on boiling water and follow the method for Rosehip Wine, opposite.
Note: Dried rosehips can be bought from home wine-making suppliers and make a wine which is as good as one made from fresh rosehips and is less trouble to prepare.

Tangerine wine

You will need for 1 gallon:

12 tangerines
4 pints boiling water
1 Campden tablet
1 teaspoon pectic
   enzyme
3 pints syrup,
   gravity 300

1 yeast nutrient
   tablet
Sauternes yeast starter
cooled, boiled water

Peel the tangerines and discard the peel.

Put the tangerines in a polythene pail and crush them well by hand. Pour over boiling water, cover and leave overnight.

Add the Campden tablet, crushed and dissolved in a little water and pectic enzyme, stir and allow to stand for 24 hours.

Add half the syrup, yeast nutrient tablet and starter and allow to ferment in a warm place for 4 days, stirring each day and replacing lid.

Strain into a 1-gallon fermentation jar, add the remaining syrup, top up to the 1-gallon mark with cooled, boiled water and fit fermentation lock.

Ferment to completion in a warm place.

Rack and mature in the usual way.

Tea wine

You will need for 1 gallon:

5 heaped teaspoons tea
5 pints boiling water
1 lb. raisins, chopped
thinly peeled rind
    1 lemon and 1 orange
juice 1 lemon and
    1 orange
3 pints syrup,
    gravity 300
1 yeast nutrient
    tablet
All-purpose wine
    yeast starter
cooled, boiled water

Make the tea in the usual way by pouring on boiling water.

When cool, put in a polythene pail with the chopped raisins, rind and juice of the orange and lemon, half the syrup, yeast nutrient tablet and starter.

Cover and allow to ferment in a warm place for 7 days, stirring each day and replacing lid.

Strain into a 1-gallon fermentation jar, add the remaining syrup, top up with cooled, boiled water and fit fermentation lock.

Rack when clear and move the wine to a cool place.

Rack again, three months later, into bottles.

Wheat wine

You will need for 1 gallon:

1 lb. wheat, washed
1 pint water
thinly peeled rind
    2 oranges and 1 lemon
2 lb. raisins
4 pints boiling water
juice 2 oranges and
    1 lemon
3½ pints syrup,
    gravity 300
1 yeast nutrient
    tablet
Tokay yeast starter
cooled, boiled water

Soak the wheat overnight in the 1 pint water.

Pour into a polythene pail and add the rinds, raisins and pour over the boiling water.

When cool, add the citrus juice, 2 pints of the syrup, yeast nutrient tablet and starter.

Cover and leave to ferment in a warm place for 14 days, stirring each day and then replacing lid.

Strain into a 1-gallon fermentation jar, add the remaining syrup, top up with cooled, boiled water and fit fermentation lock.

Rack when clear and move to a cool place.

Rack again, three months later, into bottles.

chapter 13

rosé wines

If pale pink is the colour you like your wine, the number of unmixed wines that can be made on the home front are limited.

There is no reason, however, why you should not take a white wine and mix it with a small quantity of red wine to produce the desired effect. Alternatively, you can include a small quantity of red fruit in a white wine recipe.

Gooseberry wine

You will need for 1 gallon:

4 lb. red, ripe
    gooseberries
4 pints boiling water
1 Campden tablet
1 teaspoon pectic
    enzyme
2½ pints syrup,
    gravity 300
1 yeast nutrient tablet
All-purpose wine
    yeast starter
cooled, boiled water

Top and tail the gooseberries and wash well.

Place in a polythene pail and pour over the boiling water.

When cool, crush the gooseberries by hand. Add Campden tablet, crushed and dissolved in a little water, and the pectic enzyme.

Leave covered for 3 days, crushing the fruit by hand each day.

Stir in 1½ pints of the syrup, yeast nutrient tablet and starter.

Cover and ferment for 7 days, stirring each day and then replacing lid.

Press and strain through a nylon sieve into a 1-gallon fermentation jar, add the remaining syrup and top up with cooled, boiled water to 1-gallon mark before fitting fermentation lock.

When fermentation is completed, move the wine to a cool place.

Rack, bung and bottle in the usual way.

Note: This produces a medium wine which is ready for drinking after a year. For a dry wine (drinkable after 6 months) use only 2 pints syrup; and for a sweet wine use 3 pints syrup.

Raspberry wine

You will need for 1 gallon:

2 lb. raspberries	1 yeast nutrient
5 pints cooled,	tablet
boiled water	Sauternes yeast starter
1 teaspoon pectic	2½ pints syrup,
enzyme	gravity 300
1 Campden tablet	cooled, boiled water

Wash the fruit then crush in the polythene pail. Pour over the water and add the pectic enzyme and Campden tablet, crushed and dissolved in a little water. Mix well, cover and allow to stand for 24 hours.

Add the yeast nutrient tablet and starter, cover and allow to ferment in a warm place for 4 days, stirring each day and then replacing lid.

Strain into a 1-gallon fermentation jar, add the syrup, top up with cooled, boiled water and fit fermentation lock.

Ferment to completion and then move the wine to a cool place.

Rack, bung and bottle in the usual way.

Redcurrant wine

You will need for 1 gallon:

3 lb. redcurrants	Sauternes yeast starter
5 pints boiling water	1 Campden tablet
2 teaspoons pectic	2½ pints syrup,
enzyme	gravity 300
1 yeast nutrient	cooled, boiled water
tablet	

Wash the redcurrants, strip them from their stalks and put into a polythene pail. Pour over the boiling water.

When cool, mash the redcurrants and add the pectic enzyme, yeast nutrient tablet and starter, and Campden tablet, crushed and dissolved in a little water.

Cover and allow to ferment in a warm place for 3 days, stirring each day and then replacing the lid.

Strain into a 1-gallon fermentation jar, add the syrup, top up to the 1-gallon mark with cooled, boiled water and fit fermentation lock.

Ferment to completion and then move the wine to a cool place.

Rack, bung and bottle in the usual way.

Rose petal wine

You will need for 1 gallon:

2 pints rose petals,	2½ pints syrup,
lightly pressed down	gravity 300
5 pints boiling water	1 yeast nutrient
finely grated rind and	tablet
juice 2 lemons	Sauternes yeast starter
¼ teaspoon grape	cooled, boiled water
tannin	

Wash the petals in a colander and put into a polythene pail.

Pour over 5 pints boiling water, cover and leave for 3 days, stirring each day and replacing lid.

Strain through a nylon sieve into a second polythene pail, add finely grated lemon rind, lemon juice, grape tannin, syrup, yeast nutrient tablet and starter.

Strain again a week later into a 1-gallon fermentation jar, top up to 1-gallon level with cooled, boiled water and fit fermentation lock.

Rack twice at 3-monthly intervals and then bottle.

chapter 14
meads

With a long history which stretches back to antiquity it is hardly surprising that a number of wines have been evolved from the basic fermented honey formula.

Melomels are wines made from fruit juice and honey. Two of the most famous of melomels are *Pyment*, where grapes are used, and *Cyser*, an apple-based honey wine.

Further derivatives are *Hippocras*, which is a spiced pyment and *Metheglin*, a mead to which herbs have been added.

Apricot melomel

You will need for 1 gallon:

1 lb. acacia blossom honey	1 lb. dried apricots
2 yeast nutrient tablets	1 lb. raisins, chopped
½ teaspoon Marmite	2 Campden tablets
½ oz. malic acid	Maury yeast starter
6 pints warm, boiled water	cooled, boiled water

Place the honey, nutrients and acid in a polythene pail and pour over the warm, boiled water. Add the apricots, chopped raisins and Campden tablets, crushed and dissolved in a little water. Cover and leave to stand for 24 hours.

Add the yeast starter and allow to ferment for 5 days.

Press and strain through a nylon sieve into a 1-gallon fermentation jar, top up with cooled, boiled water to 1-gallon mark, fit fermentation lock and stand in a warm place.

After about 10 days, fill the jar to the neck with cooled, boiled water and replace fermentation lock.

Rack when fermentation is complete. Rack again after about 3 months.
Bottle 6 months later.
Note: Ready to drink after a year.

Cyser

Use one of the Apple Wine recipes, page 22, substituting each 1½ lb. sugar with 2 lb. honey, and using a Maury yeast starter.

Gooseberry melomel

You will need for 1 gallon:

6 lb. gooseberries	½ teaspoon Marmite
1 lb. raisins, chopped	6 pints warm, boiled water
2 Campden tablets	
1½ lb. white honey	Maury yeast starter
2 yeast nutrient tablets	cooled, boiled water

Top and tail the gooseberries and wash well. Crush the gooseberries in a polythene pail, add chopped raisins and Campden tablets, crushed and dissolved in a little water.

Dissolve the honey and nutrients in the warm, boiled water and stir into the pail.

Allow to stand for 24 hours.

Add the yeast starter and allow to ferment for 4 days, stirring each day and then replacing lid. Press and strain through a nylon sieve into a 1-gallon fermentation jar, top up to 1-gallon mark with cooled, boiled water, fit fermentation lock and stand in a warm place.

Allow to ferment until the gravity drops to below o.

Rack, rack again after 3 months and bottle 6 months later.

Note: Ready to drink after a year.

Hippocras

You will need for 1 gallon:

2 lb. white honey
4 pints warm,
  boiled water
1 oz. root ginger
1 oz. cinnamon
4 cloves
1 pint water
1 pint white grape
  concentrate

$\frac{1}{2}$ oz. malic acid
2 yeast nutrient
  tablets
$\frac{1}{4}$ teaspoon Marmite
$\frac{1}{4}$ teaspoon grape
  tannin
2 Campden tablets
Maury yeast starter
cooled, boiled water

Dissolve the honey in the warm water in a 1-gallon fermentation jar.

Put the spices in a muslin bag and boil for 15 minutes in the 1 pint water.

When cool, strain the spiced liquid into the jar. Add the grape concentrate, acid, nutrients, tannin and Campden tablets, crushed and dissolved in a little water.

Mix well, cover and allow to stand for 24 hours.

Add the yeast starter, top up to the 1-gallon mark with cooled, boiled water, fit fermentation lock and stand in a warm place.

Ferment to dryness and then rack.

Rack again after 3 months and bottle 6 months later.

Peach melomel

You will need for 1 gallon:

7 lb. peaches
2 Campden tablets
5 pints warm,
  boiled water
2$\frac{1}{2}$ lb. clover honey
2 yeast nutrient
  tablets
$\frac{1}{4}$ teaspoon grape
  tannin

$\frac{1}{4}$ oz. tartaric acid
$\frac{1}{4}$ oz. malic acid
2 yeast nutrient
  tablets
$\frac{1}{4}$ teaspoon Marmite
Maury yeast starter
cooled, boiled water

Wipe the peaches, remove stones and put peaches into a polythene pail. Squeeze the peaches until well mashed.

Dissolve the Campden tablets in a little water and add to the peaches.

Dissolve the honey, tannin, acid and nutrients in the warm water and mix well with the peaches.
Cover and allow to stand for 24 hours.

Add the yeast starter and allow to ferment for 4 days, stirring each day and then replacing lid.

Press and strain through a nylon sieve into a 1-gallon fermentation jar, top up to 1-gallon mark with cooled, boiled water, fit fermentation lock and stand in a warm place.

When the gravity drops to 10, rack off the sediment.

Rack again when the gravity drops to 5.

Rack once more before bottling.

Note: Ready to drink after a year.

Pyment

You will need for 1 gallon:

2 lb. white honey
5 pints warm,
  boiled water
1 pint white grape
  concentrate
$\frac{1}{2}$ oz. malic acid
2 yeast nutrient tablets

$\frac{1}{4}$ teaspoon Marmite
$\frac{1}{4}$ teaspoon grape
  tannin
2 Campden tablets
Maury yeast starter
cooled, boiled water

Dissolve the honey in the warm water in a 1-gallon fermentation jar.

Add the grape concentrate, acid, nutrients, tannin and Campden tablets, crushed and dissolved in a little water.

Mix well, cover and allow to stand for 24 hours.

Add the yeast starter, top up to the 1-gallon mark with cooled, boiled water, fit fermentation lock and stand in a warm place.

Ferment to dryness and then rack.

Rack again after 3 months and bottle 6 months later.

Metheglin

You will need for 1 gallon:

3 lb. white honey
6 pints warm,
  boiled water
$\frac{1}{4}$ oz. tartaric acid
$\frac{1}{2}$ oz. malic acid
grated rind 1 lemon
3 oz. mixed dried herbs

2 yeast nutrient
  tablets
$\frac{1}{4}$ teaspoon Marmite
2 Campden tablets
Maury yeast starter
cooled, boiled water

Dissolve the honey in the warm water in a 1-gallon fermentation jar.

Add the acids, grated lemon rind, herbs, nutrients

and Campden tablets, crushed and dissolved in a little water.

Cover and allow to stand overnight.

Add the yeast starter, fit fermentation lock and ferment in a warm place for 5 days.

Strain the liquid through a nylon sieve into a second fermentation jar, top up to the 1-gallon level with cooled, boiled water, fit fermentation lock and ferment until the gravity drops to 5. Rack, rack again after 3 months and bottle 6 months later.

Blackcurrant melomel

You will need for 1 gallon:

6 lb. blackcurrants	½ teaspoon Marmite
2 Campden tablets	½ oz. malic acid
2 pints cooled, boiled water	4 pints warm, boiled water
2 lb. white honey	Maury yeast starter
2 yeast nutrient tablets	cooled, boiled water

Crush the blackcurrants in a polythene pail, stir in the Campden tablets, dissolved in a little water, and add the cooled, boiled water.

Dissolve the honey, nutrients and acid in the warm, boiled water and stir into the pail.

Cover and allow to stand for 24 hours.

Add the yeast starter and allow to ferment for 5 days, stirring each day and then replacing lid.

Press and strain through a nylon sieve into a 1-gallon fermentation jar.

Top up to 1-gallon mark with cooled, boiled water, fit fermentation lock and stand the jar in a warm place.

Allow to ferment until the gravity drops to below 0.

Rack, rack again after 3 months and bottle 6 months later.

Note:
Ready to drink after a year.

Pyment

You will need for 1 gallon:

2 lb. white honey	2 yeast nutrient tablets
5 pints warm, boiled water	¼ teaspoon Marmite
1 pint red grape concentrate	2 Campden tablets
½ oz. malic acid	Maury yeast starter
	cooled, boiled water

Dissolve the honey in the warm water in a 1-gallon fermentation jar.

Add the grape concentrate, acids, nutrients and Campden tablets, crushed and dissolved in a little water.

Mix well, cover and allow to stand for 24 hours.

Add the yeast starter, top up to the 1-gallon mark with cooled, boiled water, fit fermentation lock and stand in a warm place.

Ferment to dryness and then rack.

Rack again after 3 months and bottle 6 months later.

Raspberry melomel

You will need for 1 gallon:

2½ lb. acacia blossom honey	½ teaspoon Marmite
7 pints warm, boiled water	2 Campden tablets
5 lb. raspberries	Maury yeast starter
2 yeast nutrient tablets	½ pint red grape concentrate
	cooled, boiled water

Dissolve the honey in warm water and put into a polythene pail.

Add the raspberries, nutrients and Campden tablets, crushed and dissolved in a little water.

Stir well, cover and leave to stand for 24 hours.

Add the yeast starter and ferment for 3 days, stirring each day and then replacing lid.

Press and strain through a nylon sieve into a 1-gallon fermentation jar, add the grape concentrate, top up with cooled, boiled water to 1-gallon mark, fit fermentation lock and stand in a warm place.

Rack when fermentation is completed.

Rack again after 3 months and bottle 6 months later.

chapter 15
sparkling wines

Chapter 8 deals with the basic principles of making a sparkling wine from apples. Pears may may also be used to produce an excellent wine if the cooking variety are used. Simply substitute pears for apples in an apple wine recipe.

Two other sparkling wines have a lot to commend themselves – gooseberry and redcurrant. Gooseberry Champagne can be so good in fact that it was often fraudulently but very successfully passed off as genuine Champagne in the 19th century. Redcurrants produce an attractive light red sparkling wine.

Gooseberry wine

You will need for 1 gallon:

6 lb. unripened gooseberries
5 pints boiling water
8 oz. raisins, chopped
1 Campden tablet
1 teaspoon pectic enzyme
1 yeast nutrient tablet
Champagne yeast starter
2½ pints syrup gravity 300
cooled, boiled water

Top and tail the gooseberries and rinse in a colander. Put into a polythene pail and pour over the boiling water.

Allow to cool and then crush the berries by hand. Then add the chopped raisins, Campden tablet, crushed and dissolved in a little water, and pectic enzyme.

Allow to stand overnight.

Add the yeast nutrient tablet and starter, cover and ferment for 6 days in a warm place, pushing the fruit down each day.

Strain and press through a nylon sieve into a 1-gallon fermentation jar, add the syrup, top up to the 1-gallon mark with cooled, boiled water and fit fermentation lock.

Ferment to completion in a warm place; rack and mature.

Render the wine sparkling as described in Chapter 8, page 28.

Redcurrant wine

You will need for 1 gallon:

5 lb. redcurrants
5 pints boiling water
2 teaspoons pectic enzyme
1 yeast nutrient tablet
Champagne yeast starter
1 Campden tablet
2½ pints syrup, gravity 300
cooled, boiled water

Wash the redcurrants, strip them from their stalks and put the fruit into a polythene pail. Pour over the boiling water.

When cool, mash the redcurrants and add the pectic enzyme, yeast nutrient tablet and starter, and Campden tablet, crushed and dissolved in a little water.

Cover and allow to ferment in a warm place for 3 days, stirring each day and then replacing lid.

Strain into a 1-gallon fermentation jar, add the syrup, top up to the 1-gallon mark with cooled, boiled water and fit fermentation lock.

Ferment to completion and then move the wine to a cool place.

Rack and mature.

Render the wine sparkling as described in Chapter 8, page 28.

chapter 16
dry red wines

For those who like a glass of wine with a meal, this chapter has some very pleasant surprises in store.

Though none of these wines could replace the great Burgundies and Clarets, for every day occasions these wines will often prove superior to the cheaper red wines of doubtful origins which are commercially available. I find that home-made wines go particularly well with good, plain wholesome British cooking.

With these wines it is not difficult to produce good results and they are easy to clear to brilliance. Some of the colours are really glorious – providing you make sure that they are matured in darkness and are bottled in tinted bottles.

Beetroot and apple wine

You will need for 1 gallon:

5 pints cooled, boiled water	¼ teaspoon grape tannin
2 Campden tablets	1 yeast nutrient tablet
1 lb. beetroot	Burgundy yeast starter
8 oz. raisins, chopped	2¼ pints syrup, gravity 300
8 lb. apples	cooled, boiled water
1 teaspoon pectic enzyme	

Put the water into a polythene pail and stir in the Campden tablets, crushed and dissolved in a little water.

Wash the beetroot, peel and dice. Put them in the water and add the pectic enzyme and chopped raisins.

Wash the apples, chop, crush and put into the pail at once before they turn brown.

Cover with a lid and leave for 24 hours.

Add the grape tannin, yeast nutrient tablet and starter, ferment for 7 days, crushing the fruit by hand each day and then replacing lid.

Press and strain through a nylon sieve into a 1-gallon fermentation jar, add the syrup, top up with cooled, boiled water to 1-gallon mark and fit fermentation lock.

When fermentation is completed, move the wine to a cool place.

Rack, bung and bottle after 12 months.

Bilberry wine

You will need for 1 gallon:

3 lb. bilberries	1 Campden tablet
2 pints cooled, boiled water	1 yeast nutrient tablet
1 pint syrup, gravity 300	All-purpose wine yeast starter
1 teaspoon grape tannin	1½ pints syrup, gravity 300
1 teaspoon pectic enzyme	cooled, boiled water

Wash the bilberries and crush well in a polythene pail.

Add the 2 pints water, 1 pint syrup, tannin, pectic enzyme, Campden tablet crushed and dissolved in water, yeast nutrient tablet and starter.

Cover and ferment in a warm place for 7 days,

crushing the fruit by hand each day and then replacing lid.

Press and strain through a nylon sieve into a 1-gallon fermentation jar.

Add the syrup and top up to 1-gallon mark with cooled, boiled water.

Fit fermentation lock and ferment to dryness – about 14 days.

Rack, remove the wine to a cool place and bung.

Mature and add Campden tablet prior to bottling.

Note: Ready to drink after about a year. Serve chilled or at room temperature. Goes well with meats.

Bilberry wine

(Using canned bilberries)

You will need for 1 gallon:

15-oz. can bilberry pie filling	3 teaspoons pectic enzyme
5 pints cooled, boiled water	2¼ pints syrup, gravity 300
½ teaspoon grape tannin	1 yeast nutrient tablet
2 teaspoons citric acid	Pommard yeast starter cooled, boiled water

Mash the contents from the can of pie filling and put into a polythene pail add the water, grape tannin, citric acid and pectic enzyme.

Mix well, cover and allow to stand for 3 days, crushing the fruit by hand each day and then recovering.

Press and strain into a 1-gallon fermentation jar, add the syrup, yeast nutrient and starter, top up to 1-gallon mark with boiled water and fit fermentation lock.

Ferment to completion in a warm place.

Rack and mature in the usual way.

Blackberry and apple wine

You will need for 1 gallon:

5 pints cooled, boiled water	6 lb. cooking apples
2 Campden tablets	1 yeast nutrient tablet
2 lb. blackberries	Burgundy yeast starter
1 teaspoon pectic enzyme	2¼ pints syrup cooled, boiled water

Put the water into a polythene pail and stir in the Campden tablets, crushed and dissolved in a little water.

Wash the blackberries, crush, mix with the pectic enzyme and put into the polythene pail.

Wash the apples, chop, crush and put into the pail at once before they turn brown.

Cover with the lid and leave for 24 hours.

Add the yeast nutrient tablet and starter, ferment for 4 days, crushing the fruit by hand each day and then replacing lid.

Press and strain through a nylon sieve into a 1-gallon fermentation jar, add the syrup, top up to the 1-gallon mark with cooled, boiled water and fit fermentation lock.

When fermentation is completed, move the wine to a cool place.

Rack, bung and bottle after 12 months.

Blackberry wine

You will need for 1 gallon:

3 lb. blackberries	2½ pints syrup, gravity 300
2 pints cooled, boiled water	1 yeast nutrient tablet
2 Campden tablets	sherry yeast starter
1 teaspoon pectic enzyme	cooled, boiled water

Pick best quality, fully-ripened blackberries and crush them in a bowl with a wooden spoon.

Add the cooled, boiled water, Campden tablets, crushed and dissolved in a little water and pectic enzyme; mix thoroughly and allow to stand overnight.

Put 1 pint of the syrup into a polythene pail, strain the blackberry liquid on to it through a nylon sieve and add the yeast nutrient tablet and starter.

Cover and ferment in a warm place for 7 days, stirring each day and then replacing lid.

Pour into a 1-gallon fermentation jar, leaving behind as much sediment as possible, add remaining syrup, top up to 1-gallon mark with cooled, boiled water and fit fermentation lock. Keep the jar away from light to preserve the colour of the wine.

Rack after 3 months and bung when fermentation has finished.

Rack again after 3 months and siphon into tinted bottles.

Note: Ready for drinking after a year but there is a decided improvement with further ageing.

Blackcurrant wine

You will need for 1 gallon:

4 lb. ripe blackcurrants	2 pints syrup, gravity 300
4 pints cooled, boiled water	1 yeast nutrient tablet
1 Campden tablet	All-purpose wine yeast starter
1 teaspoon pectic enzyme	cooled, boiled water

Wash blackcurrants and crush with a wooden spoon in a polythene pail.

Pour on the cooled, boiled water and stir together

with the Campden tablet, crushed and dissolved in water, and pectic enzyme.

Leave for 2 hours.

Add 1½ pints of the syrup, yeast nutrient tablet and starter, stirring thoroughly.

Cover and ferment in a warm place for 7 days, stirring each day and then replacing lid.

Press and strain through a nylon sieve into a clean polythene pail.

Cover and ferment for another 3 days.

Leaving as much sediment behind as possible, pour into a 1-gallon fermentation jar, add the remaining syrup, top up to 1-gallon mark with cooled, boiled water and fit fermentation lock.

Rack after 3 months and bung when fermentation has stopped.

Siphon into tinted bottles to preserve colour.

Note: Drinkable after 6 months but better if kept longer.

Bullace wine

You will need for 1 gallon:

2 lb. bullaces	1 yeast nutrient
5 pints boiling water	tablet
2 Campden tablets	All-purpose wine
1 teaspoon pectic	yeast starter
enzyme	cooled, boiled water
2¼ pints syrup,	
gravity 300	

Wash the fruit and then crush to a pulp in a polythene pail. Pour on the boiling water. When cool, add the Campden tablets, crushed and dissolved in a little water, and the pectic enzyme.

Cover and allow to stand for 2 days, stirring each day and then replacing lid.

Strain through a nylon sieve into a 1-gallon fermentation jar, add the syrup, yeast nutrient tablet and starter, top up to 1-gallon level with cooled, boiled water and fit fermentation lock.

When fermentation is completed, move the wine to a cool place.

Rack, bung and bottle in the usual way.

Cherry wine

You will need for 1 gallon:

5 lb. black cherries	2½ pints syrup,
2 lb. unripened cherries	gravity 300
4 pints boiling water	1 yeast nutrient
2 Campden tablets	tablet
2 teaspoons pectic	Burgundy yeast starter
enzyme	cooled, boiled water

Remove the stalks from the cherries, wash and crush the fruit in polythene pail.

Pour over the boiling water and, when cool, add

the Campden tablets, crushed and dissolved in a little water, and the pectic enzyme. Stir well.

Leave covered for 24 hours.

Stir in the syrup, yeast nutrient tablet and starter.

Cover and ferment for 7 days, pulping the fruit by hand each day and replacing the lid.

Press and strain through nylon sieve into a 1-gallon fermentation jar and top up with cooled, boiled water to 1-gallon mark before fitting the fermentation lock.

When fermentation is completed, move the wine to a cool place.

Rack, bung and bottle in the usual way.

Note: This wine may be drunk within 6 months.

Elderberry and apple wine

You will need for 1 gallon:

5 pints cooled, boiled	2 lb. apples
water	1 yeast nutrient
2 Campden tablets	tablet
2 lb. elderberries	Burgundy yeast starter
1 teaspoon pectic	2¼ pints syrup,
enzyme	gravity 300
8 oz. raisins, chopped	cooled, boiled water

Put the water into a polythene pail and stir in the Campden tablets, crushed and dissolved in a little water. Remove the stalks from the elderberries and wash the fruit in a colander; crush them in a bowl and add to the pail, together with pectic enzyme and chopped raisins.

Wash the apples, chop, crush and put into the pail at once before they turn brown.

Cover with a lid and leave for 24 hours.

Add the yeast nutrient tablet and starter, ferment for 7 days, crushing the fruit by hand each day and then replacing lid.

Press and strain through a nylon sieve into a 1-gallon fermentation jar, add the syrup, top up with cooled, boiled water to 1-gallon mark and fit fermentation lock.

When fermentation is completed, move the wine to a cool place.

Rack, bung and bottle after 12 months.

Mixed fruit wine

You will need for 1 gallon:

1½ lb. elderberries	1 yeast nutrient
12 oz. blackberries	tablet
12 oz. redcurrants	All-purpose wine
5 pints boiling water	yeast starter
1 teaspoon pectic	2½ pints syrup,
enzyme	gravity 300
1 Campden tablet	cooled, boiled water

Wash the fruit, put into a polythene pail and pour on the boiling water.

When cool, crush the fruit by hand, add the

pectic enzyme and Campden tablet, crushed and dissolved in a little water.

Allow to stand overnight.

The next day, add the yeast nutrient tablet and starter, cover and allow to ferment in a warm place for 7 days, stirring each day and then replacing lid.

Strain into a 1-gallon fermentation jar, add the syrup, top up with cooled, boiled water and fit fermentation lock.

Ferment to completion in a warm place.

Rack and mature in a cool place.

Mulberry wine

You will need for 1 gallon:

3 lb. ripe mulberries	$\frac{1}{2}$ oz. citric acid
4 pints boiling water	1 yeast nutrient
1 Campden tablet	tablet
1 teaspoon pectic enzyme	All-purpose wine
2$\frac{1}{2}$ pints syrup,	yeast starter
gravity 300	cooled, boiled water

Wash the mulberries and put in a polythene pail. Pour on boiling water and stir in a Campden tablet, crushed and dissolved in a little water, and pectic enzyme.

Gently crush the fruit by hand.

Stir in the syrup, citric acid, yeast nutrient tablet and starter.

Cover and ferment in a warm place for 7 days, stirring each day and then replacing lid.

Strain through a nylon sieve into a 1-gallon fermentation jar, top up to 1-gallon mark with cooled, boiled water before fitting fermentation lock.

When fermentation is completed, rack, bung, mature and bottle in the usual way.

Plum wine

You will need for 1 gallon:

4 lb. red plums	2$\frac{1}{4}$ pints syrup,
1 lemon, sliced	gravity 300
5 pints cooled, boiled	1 yeast nutrient tablet
water	All-purpose wine
1 Campden tablet	yeast starter
1 teaspoon pectic enzyme	cooled, boiled water

Chop the plums, remove stones and put the fruit in a polythene pail, together with the sliced lemon.

Add the cooled, boiled water and the Campden tablet, crushed and dissolved in a little water, and pectic enzyme.

Crush the fruit by hand.

Stir in 1$\frac{1}{4}$ pints of the syrup, yeast nutrient tablet and starter.

Cover and ferment in a warm place for 10 days, stirring each day and then replacing lid.

Strain through nylon sieve into 1-gallon fermentation jar.

Add the remaining syrup and top up with cooled, boiled water before fitting fermentation lock.

When fermentation is completed, move the wine to a cool place and bung.

Rack when clear and rack again 3 months later. Siphon into bottles.

Sloe wine

You will need for 1 gallon:

3 lb. ripe sloes	1 yeast nutrient
8 oz. raisins	tablet
5 pints boiling water	Pommard yeast starter
1 Campden tablet	2$\frac{1}{4}$ pints syrup,
1 teaspoon pectic enzyme	gravity 300
1 teaspoon citric acid	cooled, boiled water

Remove the stalks and wash the sloes. Chop the raisins.

Put into a polythene pail and pour over the boiling water.

When cool, crush the sloes by hand.

Add the Campden tablet, crushed and dissolved in a little water, the pectic enzyme and citric acid. Stir well.

Cover and leave for 24 hours.

Stir in the yeast nutrient tablet and starter, cover and ferment in a warm place for 7 days, crushing the fruit by hand each day and replacing lid.

Press and strain through nylon sieve into 1-gallon fermentation jar, add the syrup and top up to 1-gallon mark with cooled, boiled water before fitting fermentation lock.

When fermentation is completed, move the wine to a cooler place.

Rack, bung and bottle in the usual way.

Note: Ready to drink after a year.

Tomato wine

You will need for 1 gallon:

7 lb. over-ripe tomatoes	1 yeast nutrient tablet
5 pints boiling water	All-purpose wine yeast starter
1 teaspoon pectic enzyme	2½ pints syrup, gravity 300
¼ teaspoon grape tannin	cooled, boiled water

Pulp the tomatoes in a polythene pail and pour on the boiling water.

When cool, add the pectic enzyme, grape tannin, yeast nutrient tablet and starter.

Cover and ferment in a warm place for 4 days, stirring well each day and then replacing lid.

Press and strain into a 1-gallon fermentation jar, add the syrup and top up to the 1-gallon mark with cooled, boiled water before fitting fermentation lock.

When fermentation is completed, move the wine to a cool place.

Rack, bung and bottle in the usual way.

Note: Ready to drink after a year.

chapter 17
sweet red wines

Most of the wines dealt with here will improve considerably by being kept for two years or more. At their best they are full bodied with a high alcohol content. In making them it is important that the fermentation does not stick otherwise they will not develop their potentially high alcohol content and the unconverted sugar will result in an excessive, unpleasant sweetness. Don't try to hurry in making these wines; allow plenty of time for fermentation and racking.

Beetroot wine

You will need for 1 gallon:

5 lb. young beetroot	juice 1 lemon
4 pints water	1 yeast nutrient tablet
thinly peeled rind 1 lemon	All-purpose wine yeast starter
3 pints syrup, gravity 300	cooled, boiled water

Wash the beetroot well and slice thinly.

Put in 4 pints cold water, bring to the boil and simmer gently for 15 minutes, together with the lemon rind.

Strain into a polythene pail, and cover.

When cool add half the syrup, the lemon juice, yeast nutrient tablet and starter.

Cover and ferment in a warm place for 6 days, stirring each day and then replacing lid.

Leaving as much sediment behind as possible, strain, through a nylon sieve, into a 1-gallon fermentation jar, add the rest of the syrup, top up to 1-gallon mark with cooled, boiled water and fit fermentation lock.

Leave in a warm place until fermentation is complete, then remove lock, bung and move the wine to a cool place.

When the wine clears rack and siphon off into tinted bottles to preserve the colour.

Beetroot and parsnip wine

You will need for 1 gallon:

3 lb. beetroot	3 pints syrup, gravity 300
3 lb. parsnips	juice 4 lemons
grated rind 4 lemons	1 yeast nutrient tablet
½ teaspoon grape tannin	All-purpose wine yeast starter
4 pints water	cooled, boiled water

Wash beetroot and parsnips; do not peel but slice thinly.

Put them in a saucepan, add the lemon rind and grape tannin and simmer for 15 minutes in 4 pints water.

Strain into polythene pail.

When cool, add half the syrup, the lemon juice, yeast nutrient tablet and starter.

Cover and ferment in a warm place for 6 days, stirring each day and then replacing lid.

Leaving as much sediment behind as possible, strain through a nylon sieve into a 1-gallon fermentation jar, add the rest of the syrup, top up to 1-gallon mark, with cooled, boiled water and fit fermentation lock.

Leave in a warm place until fermentation is completed, then remove lock, bung and move the wine to a cool place.

When the wine clears rack and siphon off into tinted bottles to preserve the colour.

Bilberry wine

You will need for 1 gallon:

2½ lb. bilberries	¼ oz. citric acid
2 pints cooled, boiled water	1 yeast nutrient tablet
3½ pints syrup, gravity 300	port wine yeast starter
½ teaspoon grape tannin	1 Campden tablet
1 teaspoon pectic enzyme	cooled, boiled water

Wash the bilberries and crush well in a polythene pail.

Add the cooled boiled water, 1 pint of the syrup, the tannin, pectic enzyme, citric acid, yeast nutrient tablet and starter, and Campden tablet crushed and dissolved in a little water.

Cover and ferment in a warm place for 7 days, crushing the fruit by hand each day and then replacing lid.

Press and strain into 1-gallon fermentation jar. Add the remaining syrup and top up to 1-gallon mark with cooled, boiled water before fitting fermentation lock.

Rack when fermentation has finished, bung and move the wine to a cool place.

Mature and add Campden tablet prior to bottling.

Note: Keep for a year or longer before drinking; makes a good after-dinner wine.

Blackberry wine

You will need for 1 gallon:

6 lb. ripe blackberries	1 yeast nutrient tablet
3 pints cooled, boiled water	Malaga wine yeast starter
1 Campden tablet	cooled, boiled water
3½ pints syrup, gravity 300	

Wash the blackberries and crush in a polythene pail and add the cooled, boiled water plus the Campden tablet crushed and dissolved in water.

Leave for 2 hours.

Add 2 pints of the syrup, the yeast nutrient tablet and starter.

Cover and ferment in a warm place for 7 days, crushing the fruit by hand each day and then replacing lid.

Press and strain into a 1-gallon fermentation jar and ferment for another 7 days with the fermentation lock in place.

Add the remaining syrup, top up to 1-gallon mark with cooled, boiled water and replace lock.

Leave in a warm place until fermentation is completed.

Rack, remove to a cool place and bung.

Bottle after about 6 months.

Note: This wine can be drunk after a year but is at its best after three years.

Blackcurrant wine

You will need for 1 gallon:

6 lb. blackcurrants	1 yeast nutrient tablet
4 pints cooled, boiled water	All-purpose wine yeast starter
1 Campden tablet	cooled, boiled water
3½ pints syrup, gravity 300	

Wash ripe fruits and crush in a polythene pail with a wooden spoon.

Pour on the cooled, boiled water and stir together with the Campden tablet, crushed and dissolved in water.

Leave for 2 hours.

Add 2 pints of the syrup, the yeast nutrient tablet and starter, stirring thoroughly.

Cover and ferment in a warm place for 7 days, stirring each day and then replacing lid.

Press and strain out solids with a nylon sieve into a second polythene pail.

Cover and ferment for another 3 days.

Leaving as much sediment behind as possible, pour into a 1-gallon fermentation jar, add the remaining syrup, top up to 1-gallon mark with cooled, boiled water and fit fermentation lock.

Rack after 3 months and bung when fermentation has finished.

Siphon off into tinted bottles to preserve colour.

Note: Drinkable after a year but better if kept longer.

Blackcurrant wine

(Using bottled syrup)

You will need for 1 gallon:

12-oz. bottle
  blackcurrant syrup
3 pints syrup,
  gravity 300
4 pints cooled, boiled
  water

½ teaspoon citric acid
1 yeast nutrient
  tablet
All-purpose yeast
  starter
cooled, boiled water

Pour the blackcurrant syrup, half the syrup and cooled, boiled water into a fermentation jar. Mix well.

Add the citric acid, yeast nutrient tablet and starter. Mix well.

Fit fermentation lock and allow to ferment in a warm place.

After 7 days, add the remaining syrup, top up to 1-gallon mark with cooled, boiled water and refit fermentation lock.

Ferment to completion and rack, bung and bottle in the usual way.

Bullace wine

You will need for 1 gallon:

4 lb. bullaces
8 oz. raisins, chopped
4 pints boiling water
1 Campden tablet
1 teaspoon pectic
  enzyme

3¼ pints syrup,
  gravity 300
1 yeast nutrient tablet
All-purpose wine
  yeast starter
cooled, boiled water

Remove the stalks, wash fruit and place in a polythene pail with the chopped raisins.

Pour over the boiling water.

When cool, mash the bullaces by hand, and add the Campden tablet, crushed and dissolved in a little water and the pectic enzyme.

Cover and leave for 4 days, mashing the fruit by hand each day and replacing lid.

Strain through a nylon sieve into a fresh polythene pail, add 2 pints of the syrup, the yeast nutrient tablet and starter. Stir well.

Cover and ferment for 7 days in a warm place, stirring each day and replacing lid.

Strain into a 1-gallon fermentation jar, add the remaining syrup and top up to 1-gallon mark with cooled, boiled water before fitting fermentation lock.

When fermentation is completed, rack into a fresh jar and move the wine to a cool place.

Rack again after three months and then bottle.

Note: Drinkable after a year.

Cherry wine

You will need for 1 gallon:

5 lb. black cherries
2 lb. unripened cherries
4 pints boiling water
2 Campden tablets
2 teaspoons pectic
  enzyme

3¼ pints syrup,
  gravity 300
1 yeast nutrient tablet
port wine yeast
  starter
cooled, boiled water

Remove the stalks from the cherries, wash the fruit and crush in a polythene pail.

Pour over the boiling water and, when cool, add the Campden tablets, crushed and dissolved in a little water, and the pectic enzyme. Stir well.

Leave covered for 24 hours.

Stir in 2 pints of the syrup, the yeast nutrient tablet and starter.

Cover and ferment for 7 days, pulping the fruit by hand each day and replacing lid.

Press and strain through a nylon sieve into a 1-gallon fermentation jar, add the remaining syrup and top up to 1-gallon mark with cooled, boiled water before fitting fermentation lock.

When fermentation is completed, move the wine to a cool place.

Rack, bung and bottle in the usual way.

Note: This wine may be drunk after 6 months but is better if kept for a year or two.

Elderberry wine

You will need for 1 gallon:

8 oz. raisins
3 lb. elderberries
3¾ pints syrup,
  gravity 300
3 pints cooled, boiled
  water

1 Campden tablet
½ oz. citric acid
1 yeast nutrient
  tablet
port yeast starter
cooled, boiled water

Chop the raisins and put them in a polythene pail with the berries, ¾ pint of the syrup, cooled, boiled water, and Campden tablet crushed and dissolved in a little water.

Stir well and leave to stand for 2 hours.

Add citric acid, yeast nutrient tablet and starter. Leave covered to ferment in a warm place for

7 days, stirring each day and then re-placing lid.
Strain and press well through a nylon sieve into a
1-gallon fermentation jar and add 1½ pints of the
syrup.

When the frothing dies down, add the remaining
syrup.

When the foam settles, top up to 1-gallon mark
with cooled, boiled water before fitting fermentation lock.

Rack when fermentation has finished after about
3 months; bung and rack again after another 3
months.

Siphon into tinted bottles.

Note: Allow wine to mature for 2 years.

Loganberry wine

You will need for 1 gallon:

6 lb. loganberries
4 pints cooled, boiled
  water
1 Campden tablet
3 pints syrup,
  gravity 300

1 yeast nutrient
  tablet
Burgundy yeast starter
cooled, boiled water

Gently wash loganberries in a colander then
put in a polythene pail.

Pour on cooled, boiled water and add Campden
tablet, crushed and dissolved in a little water.

Hand crush the fruit.

Stir in 2 pints of the syrup, the yeast nutrient
tablet and starter.

Cover and ferment in a warm place for 3 days,
crushing the fruit by hand each day and then
replacing lid.

Press and strain through nylon sieve into a
1-gallon fermentation jar, add the remaining
syrup and top up to 1-gallon mark with cooled,
boiled water before fitting fermentation lock.

Leave in a dark cupboard for 3 months, during
which time the wine should clear.

Rack, bung and rack again after 3 months,
keeping it in the dark cupboard.

Siphon into tinted bottles.

Note: May be drunk quite young but improves
after a year or two.

Mixed fruit wine

You will need for 1 gallon:

1 lb. raspberries
1 lb. blackberries
1 lb. red gooseberries
1 lb. loganberries
2 teaspoons pectic
  enzyme
2 Campden tablets

6 pints cooled, boiled
  water
1 yeast nutrient
  tablet
All-purpose yeast
  starter
cooled, boiled water

Crush the fruit in a polythene pail, add the pectic
enzyme, Campden tablets, crushed and dissolved in a little water and the water.

Cover and leave to stand for 24 hours.

Add the yeast nutrient tablet and starter, cover
and ferment in a warm place for 6 days, pressing
the fruit down each day.

Strain into a 1-gallon fermentation jar, add half
of the syrup and fit fermentation lock.

A week later, add the remaining syrup, top up to
the 1-gallon mark with cooled, boiled water and
fit fermentation lock.

Rack twice at 3-monthly intervals and mature
and bottle in the usual way.

Mulberry wine

You will need for 1 gallon:

5 lb. ripe mulberries
2 pints cooled,
  boiled water
1 Campden tablet
3 pints syrup,
  gravity 300

½ oz. citric acid
1 yeast nutrient
  tablet
port yeast starter

Wash mulberries and put in a polythene pail.

Pour on cooled, boiled water and add Campden
tablet, crushed and dissolved in a little water.

Gently crush the fruit by hand.

Stir in 1½ pints of the syrup, the citric acid, yeast
nutrient tablet and starter.

Cover and ferment in a warm place for 10 days,
stirring each day and then replacing lid.

Strain through a nylon sieve into a 1-gallon
fermentation jar, add the remaining syrup and
fit fermentation lock.

When fermentation is completed, rack, bung and
mature in the usual way.

Plum wine

You will need for 1 gallon:

4 lb. plums
1 lb. raisins
1 lemon, sliced
4 pints cooled, boiled
　　water
1 Campden tablet
3 pints syrup,
　　gravity 300

1 yeast nutrient tablet
All-purpose wine
　　yeast starter
cooled, boiled water

Cut up the plums, remove stones and put the fruit in a polythene pail, together with the raisins and sliced lemon.

Add the cooled, boiled water and the Campden tablet, crushed and dissolved in a little water.

Crush the fruit by hand.

Stir in 2 pints of the syrup, the yeast nutrient tablet and starter.

Cover and ferment in a warm place for 10 days, stirring each day and then replacing lid.

Strain through nylon sieve into 1-gallon fermentation jar, add the remaining syrup and top up with cooled, boiled water before fitting fermentation lock.

When fermentation ceases, move the wine to a cool place and bung.

Rack when clear and again 3 months later.

Siphon into bottles.

Sloe wine

You will need for 1 gallon:

3 lb. ripe sloes
8 oz. raisins
4 pints boiling water
1 Campden tablet
1 teaspoon pectic
　　enzyme

1 teaspoon citric acid
3¼ pints syrup,
　　gravity 300
1 yeast nutrient tablet
port yeast starter
cooled, boiled water

Remove the stalks and wash the sloes. Chop the raisins. Put into a polythene pail and pour over the boiling water.

When cool, crush the sloes by hand.

Add the Campden tablet, crushed and dissolved in a little water, the pectic enzyme and citric acid. Stir well, cover and leave for 24 hours.

Stir in the yeast nutrient and starter, cover and ferment in a warm place for 4 days, crushing the fruit by hand each day and replacing lid.

Stir in 2 pints of the syrup, cover, and ferment for 5 days.

Press and strain through nylon sieve into a 1-gallon fermentation jar, add the remaining syrup and top up to 1-gallon mark with cooled, boiled water before fitting fermentation lock.

When fermentation is completed, move the wine to a cool place.

Rack, bung and bottle in the usual way.

Note: Best left for 2 years before drinking.

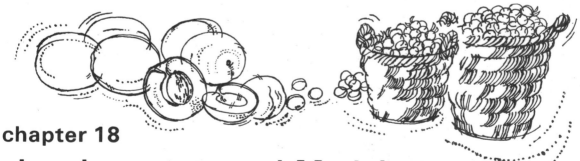

chapter 18

sherries, ports and Madeiras

Sherries, ports and Madeiras are all fortified wines i.e. wines to which spirits have been added to give them extra strength.

As stated in Chapter 9, sherry is an oxidised wine and the same is true of Madeira. Whereas, many sherries are made dry, Madeira is always made sweet.

Ports are sweet red wines which are made by the usual fermentation process – non-oxidised – and then fortified with spirit. It is best to use a neutral spirit, such as vodka, for fortification.

All these wines are fortified to give a wine with an alcohol content of between 18–22% by volume. The required level of fortification can be determined by using the Pearson Square, as described in Chapter 19.

At least 2 years is required for these wines to mature so that the full flavour has time to develop.

Apricot Madeira

You will need for 1 gallon:

2 lb. dried apricots	Madeira yeast starter
4 pints boiling water	1 pint white grape
2 teaspoons pectic	concentrate
enzyme	2½ pints syrup,
1 teaspoon citric acid	gravity 300
1 yeast nutrient	¾ pint 80° proof spirit
tablet	cooled, boiled water

Chop the apricots, put into a polythene pail and pour over the boiling water.

When cool, add the pectic enzyme, citric acid, yeast nutrient tablet and starter.

Cover and ferment in a warm place for 7 days, pressing the fruit by hand each day and then recovering.

Strain and press the fruit through a nylon sieve into a 1-gallon fermentation jar, add the grape concentrate, stir and plug lightly with cotton wool.

Add the syrup in two halves, at weekly intervals then make up to 1-gallon with cooled, boiled water.

When fermentation is finished, siphon the wine from its deposit, aerating as much as possible, into a clean fermentation jar.

Before bottling, fortify with proof spirit and mix well.

Damson port

You will need for 1 gallon:

7 lb. damsons	1 Campden tablet
4 pints boiling water	syrup, gravity 300
1½ pints red grape	1 yeast nutrient
concentrate	tablet
1 teaspoon pectic enzyme	port yeast starter
1 teaspoon citric acid	¾ pint 80° proof spirit

Wash the damsons and put into a polythene pail. Pour over the boiling water.

When cool, mash and remove the stones. Add the grape concentrate, pectic enzyme, citric acid and Campden tablet, crushed and dissolved in a little water.

Allow to stand for 24 hours.

Mash again thoroughly, draw off some of the liquid and calculate the amount of syrup and water required to bring the gravity of 1 gallon of must up to 155 (see page 22).

Do not add any syrup yet but add the yeast nutrient tablet and starter, cover, and ferment in a warm place for 7 days.

Strain into a 1-gallon fermentation jar, add half the required syrup, fit fermentation lock and ferment for 2 weeks.

Then add the second half of syrup and when fermentation ends rack into a clean jar containing the proof spirit. Rack again after two months and again into bottles after 12 months.

Parsnip sherry (sweet)

You will need for 1 gallon:

6 lb. parsnips	1 Campden tablet
4 pints boiling water	syrup, gravity 300
1½ pints white	1 yeast nutrient
grape concentrate	tablet
2 teaspoons citric acid	sherry yeast starter

Clean the parsnips, remove any blemishes and dice. Simmer in the boiling water until just tender.

Strain into a polythene pail and, when cool,

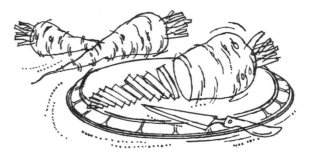

add the grape concentrate, citric acid, and Campden tablet, crushed and dissolved in a little water.

Stir well and allow to stand for 24 hours.

Calculate the amount of syrup and water to be added to produce a gallon of must with a gravity of 160 (see page 22).

Proceed as described on page 29, adding the syrup in three parts at 2-weekly intervals.

Plum sherry (dry)

You will need for 1 gallon:

4 lb. plums	syrup, gravity 300
8 oz. raisins, chopped	1 yeast nutrient
4 pints boiling water	tablet
1 teaspoon pectic enzyme	sherry yeast starter
1 Campden tablet	¾ pint 80° proof spirit

Wash the fruit, remove stones, crush the fruit in a polythene pail and add chopped raisins. Pour over the boiling water.

When cool, add the pectic enzyme and Campden tablet, crushed and dissolved in a little water.

Allow to stand for 24 hours.

Follow the rest of the procedure for producing a dry sherry, as described on page 30.

chapter 19

the Pearson Square

This chapter is devoted to the more ambitious readers – and I hope that includes many of you – who really want to grasp the basic fundamentals and principles of formulating your own wines.

I have left this bit for the latter part of the book since it might only serve to confuse the less mathematically inclined who are quite happy to follow recipes blindly.

If you're still with me, the Pearson Square is a simple formulation for you to either a) work out syrup additions or b) work out fortification calculations. We will deal with these separately.

Syrup additions

Syrup Gravity (GS)		Syrup Proportions (PS)
	Required Gravity (GR)	
Juice Gravity (GJ)		Juice Proportions (PJ)

This is how you use the Pearson Square:
1. Insert the figures for the Syrup Gravity, Juice Gravity and Required Gravity.
2. Subtract GR from GS to give PJ
i.e. $GS - GR = PJ$
3. Subtract GJ from GR to give PS
i.e. $GR - GJ = PS$
We now know the proportion of syrup of known gravity required to be added to a proportion of juice of known gravity to give the required gravity.
Now let us see how this works with an actual example. Supposing you want a gravity of 110; and that the gravity of the juice is 60 and the gravity of the syrup is 300.
We then have these known values.
GS = 300.   GR = 110.   GJ = 60

$PJ = GS - GR = 300 - 110 = 190$
$PS = GR - GJ = 110 - 60 = 50$
Therefore, 50 parts of syrup of gravity 300 have to be added to 190 parts of juice of gravity 60 to give a required gravity of 110, i.e. 5 pints of syrup to 19 pints juice. This would produce 24 pints – 3 gallons in all. For 1 gallon you would need 1.66 pints of syrup to 6.33 pints juice.

Fortification

Strength of Alcohol (SA)		Proportion of Alcohol (PA)
	Required Strength (RS)	
Strength of Wine (SW)		Proportion of Wine (PW)

The same line of calculations follows as with syrup additions:
1. Insert the figures for the Strength of Alcohol and Required Strength.
2. Subtract RS from SA to give PW
i.e. $SA - RS = PW$
3. Subtract SW from RS to give PA
i.e. $RS - SW = PA$.
We now know the proportion of alcohol of known strength required to be added to a proportion of wine of known strength to give the required strength.
Supposing you want a strength of 20°; and that the strength of the wine is 15° and the strength of the alcohol is 80°.
SA = 80. RS = 20. SW = 15
$PW = SA - RS = 60$.
$PA = RS - SW = 5$.
Therefore 5 parts of alcohol of 80° strength need to be added to 60 parts of wine of 15° strength to produce 65 parts of wine with a gravity of 20°.

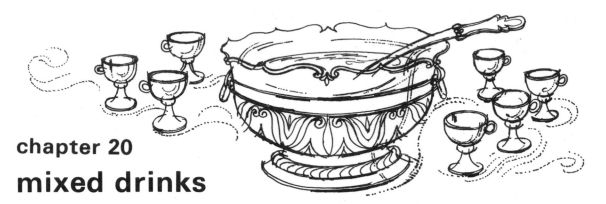

chapter 20
mixed drinks

Included here are a number of concoctions, some of which are centuries old . . . like Wassail, Bragget and Syllabub. Hot drinks for cold nights, cold drinks for hot days and some punches for parties.

It should prove interesting to try some of these drinks on your wine snob friends who turn their noses up at home-made wines. Under camouflage, it is doubtful whether the home-made qualities of the wines will be apparent to them. Again, at parties it might be considered *infra dig* to offer your guests home-made wines. But if you're entertaining on any sort of scale, the punches will prove inexpensive with their home-made wines base and will go down extremely well.

Bragget

You will need for about 2 pints:

1 tablespoon honey	1 tablespoon boiling
1 teaspoon cinnamon	water
3 cloves	2 pints strong ale

Mix the honey, cinnamon, cloves and water. Heat the ale until just warm, add the honey mixture and mix well. Drink hot.

Brown caudle

You will need for about 1 pint:

1 pint beer	juice 1 lemon
1 tablespoon oatmeal	pinch cinnamon
sugar to taste	1–2 tablespoons whisky

Warm the beer and pour it over the oatmeal. Allow to stand for a few hours and then strain. Add the rest of the ingredients.

Buttered ale

You will need for about 1 pint:

4 oz. butter	1 pint ale

Soften the butter (do not melt it). Warm the beer then pour over the butter, stirring briskly.

Caudle

You will need for about 2 pints:

1 egg white	1 pint water
6 egg yolks	8 oz. sugar
1 bottle white wine	grated rind 1 lemon

Whisk the egg white and yolks to a froth and then whisk in the rest of the ingredients. Put in the top of a double boiler and whisk until the mixture thickens. Serve immediately.

White caudle

You will need for about 5 pints:

4 pints water	pinch ground ginger
4 tablespoons oatmeal	1 bottle white wine
grated rind 1 lemon	sugar to taste
2 cloves	

Simmer all the ingredients, except the wine and sugar, together for 1 hour, stirring from time to time. Strain on to the white wine, add sugar to taste, and serve hot.

Champagne cup

You will need for about 2 pints:

thinly peeled rind	1 bottle sparkling
Seville orange	white wine
slices cucumber,	2–3 tablespoons brandy
apricot, pineapple	iced soda water

Chill the fruit and cucumber in the refrigerator. Add the wine, brandy and soda water.

Cider cup

You will need for 3 pints:

2 tablespoons sugar
grated rind and juice
  1 lemon
1–2 tablespoons brandy
slices cucumber
2 pints cider
1 pint soda water

Chill the sugar, lemon rind and juice and brandy.
Add the cucumber, cider and soda water.

Claret cup

You will need for about 3 pints:

1 bottle dry red wine
1 bottle lemonade
4 tablespoons sugar
½ teaspoon grated
  nutmeg
sprig green borage
8 oz. crushed ice

Mix all the ingredients in a large glass jug and
then serve.

Egg nog

You will need for about ½ pint:

2 egg yolks
2 tablespoons boiling
  water
1 tablespoon castor
  sugar
¼ pint cream
¼ pint sherry

Beat the egg yolks and water until frothy, then
beat in the sugar and cream. When frothy, beat
in the sherry.

Elderberry negus

You will need for about 3 pints:

brown sugar to taste
2 cloves
1 teaspoon ground
  ginger
grated rind and juice
  1 lemon
2 pints water
1 bottle elderberry
  wine
1–2 tablespoons brandy

Place the sugar, cloves, ginger and lemon rind
and juice in a saucepan with the water and bring
to the boil and simmer for 5 minutes. Warm the
wine and add to the other ingredients together
with the brandy. Serve hot.

Floster

You will need for about 2 pints:

¼ pint dry white wine
1 tablespoon sugar
2 slices lemon
4 tablespoons brandy
iced soda water

Mix all the ingredients and serve cold.

French mulled wine

You will need for about 1 pint:

¼ teaspoon mixed spice
¼ teaspoon cinnamon
¼ teaspoon ginger
6 cloves
strip lemon peel
3 oz. sugar
¼ pint water
1 pint red wine

Place the spices, sugar and water in a saucepan.
Bring to the boil, add the wine, heat and serve.

Guards cup

You will need for about 1 gallon:

½ bottle sherry
½ bottle perry
1 bottle cider
½ pint brandy
4 pints water
1 bottle sparkling
  white wine
sprig borage

Mix the sherry, perry and cider. Add the
brandy and water. Pour in the wine. Add the
borage and serve cold.

Cucumber cup

You will need for about 2 pints:

¼ cucumber, sliced
2 tablespoons castor
  sugar
thinly peeled rind
  1 lemon
3 tablespoons brandy
6 tablespoons white
  wine
1 bottle red wine
1 syphon soda
crushed ice

Macerate the first three ingredients with a
wooden spoon. Add the remaining ingredients,
except the ice, put in a bowl and allow to stand
for 1 hour. Add crushed ice and liven up with
more soda water before serving.

Het pint

You will need for about 4 pints:

3 bottles dry
  white wine
¼ teaspoon freshly
  grated nutmeg
1 tablespoon sugar
3 eggs
½ bottle whisky

Heat the wine to near boiling then add the
nutmeg and sugar. Remove from the heat,
whisk the eggs then beat into the wine mixture,
taking care not to let it curdle. Beat in the whisky
and serve at once.

Imperial punch

You will need for about 4 pints:

1 pineapple,
  thinly sliced
4 sweet oranges,
  peeled and sliced
pinch cinnamon
grated rind and juice
  1 lemon
6 sugar lumps

2 pints hot water
1 bottle rum
1 bottle sweet
  white wine
1 bottle dry
  white wine
soda water

Put the pineapple and oranges into a punch bowl and add the cinnamon. Put the lemon rind and juice with the sugar, dissolve in the hot water and add to punch bowl. When cold, add the rum and wine. Chill in the refrigerator. Liven up with soda water just before serving.

Lamb's wool

You will need for about 6 pints:

8 oz. honey
6 pints warm beer
¼ teaspoon grated
  nutmeg

¼ teaspoon ground
  ginger

Dissolve the honey in 1 pint of the warm beer, stir and add the nutmeg and ginger. Allow to stand for a while then add the remaining warm beer.

White wine cup

You will need for about 2 pints:

plenty of ice
6 slices cucumber
grated rind and juice
  1 lemon

2 tablespoons sugar
1 bottle dry white
  wine
1 bottle soda water

Put the ice, cucumber, lemon rind and juice and sugar in a jug. Add the wine and soda water.

Mulled ale

You will need for about 2 pints:

2 pints ale
1 tablespoon sugar
4 cloves

pinch nutmeg
1–2 tablespoons
  brandy

Heat the ale with the sugar, cloves and nutmeg. Pour into a warm jug and add the brandy.

Mulled red wine

You will need for about 4 pints:

6 cloves
pinch cinnamon
thinly peeled rind
  ½ lemon
2 slices lemon
4 oz. castor sugar

1 pint water
¼ teaspoon freshly
  grated nutmeg
2 bottles red wine
1–2 tablespoons brandy

Boil the cloves, cinnamon, lemon rind and sugar in the water for 15 minutes, then add the rest of the ingredients. Strain then serve hot.

Negus

You will need for about 3½ pints:

1 bottle red wine
10 sugar lumps
1 lemon
¼ teaspoon freshly
  grated nutmeg

2 pints boiling water
2–3 tablespoons brandy

Heat the red wine. Rub the sugar lumps with the lemon until well impregnated with the zest. Add to the wine, squeeze in the lemon juice and add the nutmeg. Mix well, add boiling water and brandy. Serve hot.

Syllabub

You will need for about 1 pint:

6 sugar lumps
1 lemon
3 tablespoons brandy
1 bottle sweet
  white wine

1 egg white
1 pint double cream

Rub the sugar lumps over the lemon to absorb the zest and mix with the brandy and wine. Beat the egg white until stiff, whip the cream and gradually stir into the egg white. Add to the wine and whisk until blended. Put into the refrigerator and serve the next day.

Turk's blood

You will need for about 3 pints:

¼ pint rum
1 bottle sweet
  red wine

1 bottle sparkling
  white wine

Put the rum into a punch bowl and add the red wine. Stir then add the sparkling wine just before serving.

Wassail

You will need for about 9 pints:

8 pints beer
8 oz. honey
¼ teaspoon freshly
 grated nutmeg

6 cloves
4 baked apples
1 bottle dry white
 wine

Warm the beer and pour over the honey, nutmeg and cloves. Stir until mixed. Add the whole baked apples.
When cool, add the wine.
Allow the wassail to stand for a few hours before drinking for the flavours to blend.

chapter 21
making beers in larger quantities

After your first trial run in making a beer, you will most likely have found that you can drink it in a fraction of the time it has taken you to make it. If, as I hope, you intend to go on making beer you will find that it is almost as quick to make up four or five gallons of beer at a time as it is to make up one gallon. You may also find it worth your while to make authentic beers and stouts from malt instead of malt extract. This undoubtedly produces better quality beers and if you are going to concentrate on producing beer in any quantity, you should equip yourself accordingly.

EQUIPMENT FOR LARGER SCALE PRODUCTION
A 7-gallon electric or gas wash boiler or aluminium boiler.
A 5-gallon polythene dustbin.
A 50-watt glass immersion heater.

Mashing

When making beer from malt, the malt has to be subjected to a process called mashing to convert the starch into maltose or sugar. The success of this operation is of central importance in producing a good beer and it depends on accurate temperature control.

There are two ways of doing this: using a 5-gallon polythene dustbin with lid and a 50-watt glass immersion heater; or with a small electric boiler fitted with a thermostat. The temperature can then be maintained between 130–150°F. for a number of hours ensuring a good extraction without overheating.

Testing for completion of mashing

The object of mashing is to convert all the starch into sugar. The presence of starch is easily detected in the wort by testing with a solution of tincture of iodine diluted with an equal quantity of water. All you do is to put a few drops of the brew into a cup and add a drop of the iodine solution. The mixture will turn blue if there is any starch present. In this case you should continue mashing until the iodine test is negative.

Priming tap jars and barrels

Leave about a ½-gallon space at the top for any pressure that may build up after priming.
Use 3 oz. syrup, gravity 300, for each 4 gallons, if all the sugar has been fermented (first carry out Clinitest procedure, as described on page 19, and make adjustment to syrup addition accordingly, if necessary).

Experimenting

As was mentioned in Chapter 2, there are literally hundreds of different recipes for beers. A few are included here, based on malt, which may or may not be exactly to your taste. In which case, slightly alter the quantities of ingredients and you

71

may make a beer which is more to your liking. Use more sugar and this will result in increased strength but at the same time you will get a thinner beer. You are the final arbiter on taste so it is up to you.

Lager

You will need for 4 gallons:

4 gallons water
4 lb. pale malt
pale ale water treatment, if necessary

2 oz. German hops
2¾ lb. sugar
½ teaspoon citric acid
lager yeast starter

Heat 2 gallons of the water to 150°F. Crack the malt and put into a 2-gallon polythene pail and add as much of the water as you can. Retain any remaining water for subsequent addition.

Put the 50-watt immersion heater into the pail, cover and place a blanket over the pail to retain the heat. Leave the heater on for about 8 hours.

Test that all the starch has been converted then strain into a boiler. Add the remaining water from the first 2 gallons together with the hops. Bring to the boil and simmer gently for 45 minutes.

Strain the wort on to the sugar and citric acid in a polythene dustbin. Add another 2 gallons of water, stir until all the sugar is dissolved, and add the yeast starter when the temperature drops to 60°F.

Ferment for 7 days in a warm place, skimming off any froth after 2 days.

Bottle when the gravity is about 7, priming if necessary.

Bitter

You will need for 4 gallons:

6 lb. pale malt
6 oz. crystal malt
4 gallons water
pale ale water treatment, if necessary

2 oz. Goldings hops
2 lb. glucose chips
beer yeast starter

Crack the malts and mash as described in the lager recipe, above.

Test that all the starch has been converted then strain into a boiler. Add the remaining water from the first 2 gallons and a further 2 gallons, plus the hops and glucose chippings. Bring to the boil and allow to simmer for 1½ hours.

Strain the wort into a polythene dustbin and pitch with the yeast when the temperature drops to 60°F.

Allow to ferment in a warm place until the

gravity drops to 10, skimming the froth off after the first day.

Rack, prime and bottle in the usual way.

Mild ale

You will need for 4 gallons:

4 lb. crystal malt
1¼ lb. flaked maize
4 gallons water
mild ale water treatment, if necessary

3 oz. Fuggles hops
2 teaspoons caramel
4 lb. Demerara sugar
1 teaspoon citric acid
beer yeast starter

Crack the malt and mash with the maize as described in the lager recipe, opposite.

Test that all the starch has been converted then strain into a boiler. Add the remaining water from the first 2 gallons and the hops, and simmer for 45 minutes. Simmer for a further 5 minutes with the caramel.

Strain the wort on to the sugar and citric acid in a polythene dustbin. Add another 2 gallons water, stir until all the sugar is dissolved and add the yeast when the temperature drops to 60°F.

Allow to ferment in a warm place, skim off the froth after the first day, and leave for about 10 days until the gravity is below 10.

Rack into bottles and prime, if necessary.

Stout

You will need for 4 gallons:

4 lb. pale malt
2 lb. crystal malt
1 lb. black malt
4 gallons water

3 oz. Fuggles hops
2¼ lb. sugar
½ teaspoon citric acid
beer yeast starter

Crack the malts and mash as described in the lager recipe, opposite.

Test that all the starch has been converted then strain into a boiler. Add the remaining water from the first 2 gallons and the hops.

Simmer for 45 minutes.

Strain the wort on to the sugar and citric acid in a polythene dustbin. Add another 2 gallons of water, stir until all the sugar is dissolved and pitch with the yeast when the temperature drops to 60°F.

Allow to ferment in a warm place for about 8 days, skimming off the foam after 2 days.

When the gravity drops below 10, rack into bottles and prime, if necessary.

Milk stout

You will need for 1 gallon:

2 lb. black malt
8 oz. flaked barley
4 gallons water
mild ale water treatment,
   if necessary

3 oz. Fuggles hops
2 lb. glucose
beer yeast starter
8 oz. lactose

Crack the malt and mash with the barley as described in the lager recipe, page 72.

Add the remaining water from the first 2 gallons and the hops, and simmer for 45 minutes.

Strain the wort on to the glucose in a polythene dustbin. Add another 2 gallons of water, stir until all the glucose is dissolved and pitch with the yeast when the temperature drops to 60° F.

Allow to ferment in a warm place, skim on the third day and leave for about 10 days until the gravity drops to below 10.

Add the lactose (non-fermentable) and stir well. Rack into bottles and prime, if necessary.

Cider

It is not worth the effort of making cider unless you have a fruit press and the apples are cheap and in plentiful supply. The type of apple is important too. Cider apples are, of course ideal but bitter sweet apples of any variety can be used. Alternatively, one part of cooking apples can be mixed with two parts of bitter sweet apples.

Allow 1 Campden tablet per gallon of extracted juice and ferment with a Champagne yeast starter. No yeast nutrient is necessary.

The cider should be racked when the gravity has dropped to from 5–10, to produce a dry cider which sparkles.

For a sweet cider, perhaps the easiest way is to add some syrup just before it is drunk.

The cider should be racked into casks and left to mature from three to six months before drinking. Bottling is not recommended for the home brewer since the bottles can very easily explode if there is renewed fermentation.

Perry

This is produced from pears – special perry pears – in a similar manner to making cider. 2 teaspoons of yeast nutrient should be added to each gallon. A sweet perry can be made by racking when the gravity drops by one third.

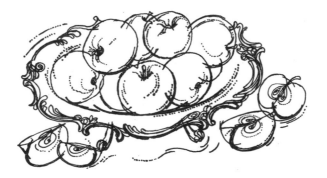

index

acknowledgements

Cover photograph by Roy Rich of Angel Studio
Fruit press photograph on page 21 by kind permission of W. R. Loftus,
1–3 Charlotte Street, London, W.1 and 16 The Terrace, Fleet Street,
Torquay.

The author and publishers would like to extend their grateful thanks
to W. R. Loftus for lending the equipment used in the photographs and
for their help and advice.

Illustrated by Jackie Grippaudo

© The Hamlyn Publishing Group Limited 1971
ISBN 0 600 34358 8
Published by The Hamlyn Publishing Group Limited
London · New York · Sydney · Toronto
Hamlyn House, Feltham, Middlesex, England
Filmset by Filmtype Services Limited, Scarborough
Printed by Litografia A. Romero S.A. Santa Cruz de Tenerife,
Canary Islands (Spain)